Rob Silverstone spent many years cooking in Oxford, Copenhagen and Nice. A keen interest in healthy eating led to collaboration with the eminent French chef Michel Guérard, author of 'Cuisine Minceur'. In 1994 he opened 'The Cook and Fiddle' on Brighton seafront, using fish from the fishermen, local cheeses and Cuckmere Valley wine. The abundance of Normandy markets tempted him to try a restaurant in Rouen. The gothic architecture of the old quarter inspired a passion for black and white photography. His pictures have been exhibited in Brighton and at 'Photofolies' in the Loire.

# A MULE IN BRIGHTON

## A Taste of The Downs

# Rob Silverstone

A MULE IN BRIGHTON

A Taste of The Downs

Vanguard Press

VANGUARD PAPERBACK

© Copyright 2007
**Rob Silverstone**

The right of Rob Silverstone to be identified as author of this work has been asserted by him in accordance with the Copyright, Designs and Patents Act 1988.

**All Rights Reserved**

No reproduction, copy or transmission of this publication may be made without written permission.
No paragraph of this publication may be reproduced, copied or transmitted save with the written permission of the publisher, or in accordance with the provisions of the Copyright Act 1956 (as amended).

Any person who commits any unauthorised act in relation to this publication may be liable to criminal prosecution and civil claims for damages.

A CIP catalogue record for this title is available from the British Library.

The map is reproduced from the Brighton & Lewes Ordnance Survey map Scale 3 miles to 1 inch by permission of Ordnance Survey on behalf of The Controller of Her Majesty's Stationery Office.© Crown copyright. All rights reserved. Licence number WL9610

ISBN 978 1 84386 310 6

*Vanguard Press is an imprint of
Pegasus Elliot MacKenzie Publishers Ltd.*
**www.pegasuspublishers.com**

First Published in 2007

**Vanguard Press
Sheraton House  Castle Park
Cambridge  England**

Printed & Bound in Great Britain

# Dedication

To the "Cook and Fiddle" brigade.

Carrie, Maggie, Jim, Ben, Leek and Pierre.

By the same author

**A Mule in Rouen - A Discovery of Upper Normandy**
ISBN 978-1-84386-163-8

'The secrets of Normandy countryside discovered by bike, and the tale of a Brighton chef setting up shop in France'.

Read more adventures of the Mule, including another chapter on Brighton.

'If you enjoyed Peter Mayles 'A Year in Provence' you're bound to like this similar account of Rob Silverstones' experience in Normandy'.

*The Brighton Argus*

'An excellent read. Silverstones' engaging account of setting up a restaurant in Normandy is a reminder that not all plans run smoothly. What he lacks in luck as an entrepreneur he certainly makes up for as a writer'.

*Everything France*

'An engaging diary-cum-travel log written in a pleasing, informal style. Travelling largely by bicycle through Normandy, Silverstone can make a bar redolent of Edith Piaf with a short, evocative turn of phrase. He is at his best when reading Flaubert's Madame Bovary and drawing perceptive comparisons with what he sees around him'.

*The Sussex Express*

# Contents

| | |
|---|---|
| Lost in Hove | 15 |
| Bicycle Days | 22 |
| A Happy Camel | 31 |
| The Royal Pavilion | 38 |
| Festival Nights | 46 |
| Heritage Sussex | 53 |
| Seagull City | 63 |
| Photographs | 71 |
| Cooking Under The Arches | 135 |
| Local Food Directory | 187 |
| Cycle routes | 195 |

## Lost in Hove

A new routine takes me across Brighton to Deepest Hove. Up and over the mighty hill on the Ditchling Road, I take up position on the platform at London Road and await the shiny green capsule that glides over the viaduct into the vast atrium of girder and glass that is Brighton station. The doors bleep open and the human cargo, hitherto silent and still, bursts onto the platform, a cavalcade of suits making for the connection to London Town. A less ambitious bunch board the little chugger that stops a hundred times on the coastway West to Pompey. Through the tunnel to Hove station, a place of peeling charm, a fading reminder that Senior Service satisfies, and the erstwhile Perfumery Company, still extolling in mosaic flourish,

'Dubarrys' Cream Shalimar for dainty soft white hands
Silkshave soap for a luxurious shave.'

On past great heaps of coal to Aldrington. I cycle down the deserted platform to the Portland Road which caters for every part of the anatomy. The Eternal Dress Agency, Hidden Hearing, The Nut and Bolt Shop. Then you're into coastal Hove, flat and featureless as an urban Fen, all the colour and excess of Brighton prohibited by decree, just a sea of solid houses, stiff with net curtains. Down one such street, a little parade of shops preserved in time. Butcher, clockmaker, poodle parlour, and most recent arrival, my 'Little Farmhouse Deli'.

Open up the shop, bustle about the kitchen and wait for custom to appear. There is a lot of waiting and watching. Plenty of aged folk with every form of walking apparel, one stick, two sticks, the three-pronged rolling zimmer and the deluxe shiny scooter with shopping bag at the rear. Plenty of grotesques who heave their sagging tracksuit bodies out of the car, into the fishmonger's opposite, the door creaking open and shut like a stubborn coffin lid. Occasionally a friendly figure does appear across my portal, expressing delight at the spread of homemade produce. Pearls to savour. The shop is presided over by Sir Hugh Clodd, who guides the customer over the selection of Sussex cheeses and the lustrous olives borne from a Peloponnesian hillside on the back of a free-range donkey. 'Cloddy' has a few features not immediately synonymous with a pristine food handler. Hard rock stubble, a perpetual running nose, his beak cloth not a thing of beauty. Often arriving grey about the gills, slumping down at the back of the shop, and clasping his bone head dolefully before he bemoans, 'Me be so hung over'. A kilo of coffee later, he is back to speed with the bagel knife, repartee and good humour.

The afternoon slides away, I put the display cabinet to bed and make for home. Aldrington is not really a station, just a platform propped on flimsy concrete leggings, with a tiny sentry box steeped in piss, scant protection against the inferno of a passing express. Gulag fencing confines the view to an unchanging stretch of track. Every evening the same figures materialise on the platform and silently lay claim to a space, stoically absorbing the metallic announcements without any discernible rage. A trackside fire, a marauding cow, vandals on the line, nothing can induce a collective show of dissent, an amused sharing of the English condition. One scorching day, the air so still, the signal burning stubbornly red, a luminous orange railway jacket came ambling up the track, and you knew that a survivor of Chernobyl on a broken crutch would reach Brighton quicker than the train.

\*\*\*

Even before opening to the public, an aged totterer cursed the very threshold of the shop. 'This is terrible. This is terrible. I shall never get in', guttural condemnation hanging from her beak. Not irredeemably deterred though. When later I introduced a two tier step, she appeared, a picture of delight. 'I can get in now!' commanding honey, focaccia and taramasalata with carefree delight. And there's Elsie with a sparkling eye and cock of the head. Always game for something new, hazelnut cheesecake or a slice of garlic sausage. Then it's back to the home where a horseshoe of residents are propped senseless in their chairs. Marge, my favourite old timer, has unfortunately been in dry dock for repairs to the knee. She started off in a shiny little ward where 'It was wonderful, we were only three to a bed.' Was dispatched unceremoniously to the workhouse on the hill. 'Eighteen old biddies filing past my left ear to the toilet each night. Anyway. I've made a start at walking with a zither.'

To the outside world, the parade where I pass my days

stands proud as the past. Wicker shopping baskets bustling like bees between the florist, clockmaker and cheery butcher, all manner of waving and greeting dispensed across the street. It is that cold, white English past, where pain and loathing is concealed like shrapnel lodged in the hip. Today, amidst much shrill cooing, a plummy lady settled her parents down for a bite of lunch. The awful authority of their accents now diminished by woolly deafness and wayward feet. After the munching was complete, and the bill paid without an iota of a tip, the tall, lean father-figure managed to pitch head first out into the street. As he picked himself up in spindly fashion the womenfolk, curiously indisposed to help, turned to each other, an edge of disappointment in the voice, 'No, not a proper fall this time.'

Recently the train journey has also taken on the soundtrack of the past, one platform announcing in schoolmasterly black ink, the other responding in the clipped female tones of a croupier pushing battleships about the North Sea. One day a crossed line will finally allow that brave little lady to speak to the nice gent, accepting his offer to tea. Best not to make the rendezvous by rail. Today, just nudging through the tunnel beneath the Seven Dials, the old slam door chugger expired within sight of home. After much commotion from ruddy-faced loco men, it transpired that the old beauty still had it in her to run in reverse, and we slid slowly back to Hove.

***

Empty stretches of school holidays unwound in the food

warehouse, the family business for close on a hundred years. Long dark gangways piled high with every conceivable condiment, destined for neighbourhood shops that still sliced ham on the bone, measured tea on scales and coaxed down packages of shredded wheat with a canny clasping pole. At home, the founding fathers who ran the warehouse were versed in the Old Testament, dispensing advice to the young folk with an avuncular tweak of the cheek. At the 'ware 'arse' they were transformed into hunched figures of hate, locked in a round of shouting and swearing that caused the air to wilt. A colossus of a man, stiffened but still stronger than a forklift truck, carted the goods onto a ramshackle lorry, sweat powering from his body like a radioactive core. The warehouse should have relocated my life to a sun-drenched hammock beneath coconut trees, semaphore signals rising contentedly from a cigar. Jack Cohen, founder of Tesco's, asked my grandpappy to supply his chain of 'supermarkets', a new concept he was importing from the States. He must have considered the offer, held a shouting summit at Chicksand Street, then decided to turn Jack Cohen down.

Well, a new Tesco has arisen in Hove, on the poisoned ground of a gasworks, hoovering up custom from miles around. I can no longer afford Sir Hugh Clodd, and must endure the twilight world of West Hove without the daily joust of humour. Grim determination carries the populace through their days. Richly painted faces come rattling through the chemist's door, lone men, lights out, clasping their morning bottle of wine. A bulldog woman with goggles scoots by on a motorised chariot, a zimmer frame rammed over her head. This is a cold comfort world that never knew

The Beatles or went barefoot on the beach. People who clothe their dogs in exquisite coats but yield no human warmth, who slip anonymous messages through your letter box at night.

\*\*\*

The Albanians are back. All winter they laboured on a big house conversion, departing the shop every day with a steaming tower of polystyrene cups. Impeccably well-mannered, stamping their muddy boots on the mat, they were soon fluent in builders' patter. 'Just a few bits and bobs to do, then the job's done and dusted', sounds faintly magical in an Albanian accent. Dispels all thoughts of barricading the ports and rolling back the sea. Planning permission has been granted for an attic flat, so they're back rampaging about the roof. The big shy one, not content with a day bulldozing walls with his bare hands, attends the gym morning and night. His physique rolls down the street in a ripple of lithe muscle. Anyway, last night he attempted a dumb-bell too far, and the weight crashed down on his neck, enough to cripple you or me. Well, he's turned up to work today with a humungously ricked neck, advancing gingerly down the street with the look of a craning tortoise.

But then, by something greater than a miracle, an Italian buys my shop. Shower this man with golden salamis and singing prosciutto, let a crowd stampede his deli counter, each customer charmed by the Tuscan greeting into parting with her purse. 'And now young lady...I have something special for you today!' The patter, something I physically could not perform. I am a chef happy in his kitchen, for whom customers are an alien presence. As an old critter departs the shop with <u>six</u> olives and <u>two</u> slices of ham, I finally pull up the drawbridge and disconnect from this becalmed backwater of Hove. Galloping carefree back to Brighton, the Mule is once more free.

\*\*\*

## Bicycle Days

Sunshine diminishes the impetus to find work. Days of vacant happiness drifting among the thousand coffee shops that populate Brighton streets. To make sense of the world reformed in the image of a coffee bean, you have to be selective. Avoid anything remotely franchised, anywhere crackling with discordant radio or terraces glinting with tubular metal chairs. This reduces the choice to about three. I initially avoided the 'Red Roaster' as it used to be the Kemptown Post Office, and signified the demise of the last few useful shops in town. Foolish Neanderthal that I am. Who needs counter clerks pounding out alms to the poor when they can be fed via electronic tagging? Far better to have transformed the premises into this vast salon bustling with exuberant faces, young media types manipulating their phones and papers with panache, strangely familiar eccentrics hovering somewhere between genius and despair, eyes locked in thoughts that finally evaporate in a fug of smoke. The coffee beans are roasted in a huge hopper, precursor to the ceremonial frothing of the milk, pulverised and beaten into shape, finally appearing on the surface of the cup in the sculpted image of a Fleur de Lys, Madonna, Saint George slaying the dragon. Artistry in the eye of the consumer.

The staff generates bonhomie with leisured, natural

smiles, but thus far I have not progressed to an exchange of names. At 'Café Motu' in Trafalgar Street, it is Pete and Jacquie. Pete works seamlessly with the dumb waiter, and maintains an exclusive insight into the transfer dealings at The Spurs, every machination of the Board relayed through no less a figure than The Window Cleaner. Jacquie provides the entire repertoire of bacon and eggs, as well as a goats cheese salad scented with lavender and spun with golden honey. The coffee is good, but in my experience, an Italian hand on the espresso machine produces an unparalleled cup. Three years teaching in Bournemouth were salvaged by nightly visits to 'Il Mondo', where a single sip of cappuccino was like mainlining neat caffeine. A second cup stopped you sleeping for a week. But you had to have it.... and then a third, eyes spinning in their sockets as Alex carried pizzas high above the babble of foreign tongues. Take the bridleway behind Brighton racecourse, past the windmill, and you arrive at a tiny Italian café on the slip road to Rottingdean beach. 'Itsa lovely day. Don'ta be sad, be happy', loses its appeal when ground out for the hundredth time, but the coffee is mega, and the poached eggs on toast an old time treat.

Rottingdean beach epitomises the English seaside. A hip-hop pebble dash into the waves, rock pools between the groynes, and more painful still, family life exposed for all to see. Every maternal command a fearsome constraint.

'Don't you start.'

'Don't sit under the cliff.'

'Don't pull that willy. You don't know where it's been.'

Across the road, into the village, everything is as it ever was. A master butchers, timbered teashops and windows crammed with antiques. Insatiable demand for copper bed warmers on a stick. Wandered through the cloistered opening to the Kipling Gardens, a succession of stone enclosures capturing simple states of bliss. A huge rose bed bursting with scent. A perfectly coiffured croquet lawn, the wooden 'clock' of a hammer, and the ball wandering off in a world of its own. Returning through Ovingdean I entered the yard of a very strict church. 'Plastic flowers will be removed and destroyed. Be sure to bolt the Lynch Gate. The full set of 'Graveyard Rules' available from the warden.'

Why the need for legislation? People come, realise there's nothing to nick and depart. Carried on up and round the racetrack, then down through Whitehawk, an estate trapped in a cleft of The Downs. The 'Black Rock Bait Shop' offers boat trips aboard 'The Lady of The Lake', and an eclectic mix of sales. Birdseed, barbecues and fireworks, all delivered to your door in a vintage Austin Morris van. What more could you want in life? Polly fed and chargrilled fish beneath a pyrotechnic sky.

\*\*\*

Boarded the 'Transmanche' at Newhaven and floated back to Normandy. The old familiar train from Dieppe swept along the valley of the Scie, deeply verdant after weeks of rain, the apple blossom piled into snowdrifts. Through the station concourse at Rouen, a majestic arc of light and sound, into the Café Metropole to find Christophe and Lorette sparkling with delight. Some things have changed. The cathedral has finally shed its scaffolding, the square now too tiny to contain its unblemished splendour. And the streets are no longer strewn with dog shit, a disorientating development as I am used to walking about Rouen with one eye pointing forward, the other scouring the cobblestones like a searchlight. I remember a man nonchalantly standing sentry as his dog performed on my doorstep, a look of strenuous intensity on its face, like a commis chef piping a profiterole. Part of the same birthright that entitles a Frenchman to waft cigarette smoke down your throat, just as you tuck into dinner, the fug rising to reveal a plate of oozing red meat, adorned with a single baby carrot. But what is this? A poster advertising a Veggie Pride march to Paris. The national identity in tatters.

Normans are proudly territorial, everyone scouring their local paper each day as if in direct communion with the oracle. I remember reading about a concierge who had unwittingly solved a burglary as he rummaged through the wheelybins for evidence of the underside of his tenants' lives. One day he unearthed a swag bag that had been deposited in haste, the scent on the booty matched that of a local hoodlum, et voilà, one burglar behind bars, the streets safer, and if every concierge shared the same sense of civic duty, we could all leave our doors unlocked and sit round the hearth rosy-cheeked, papa playing the mandolin, mami spinning wool in the corner. In Brighton there is no need for concierges, the seagulls sift through our rubbish in brazen-beaked manner. The other day I caught one rattling my dustbin lid like a wifey during a hunger strike. Totally undeterred by my presence, he drained every plastic container of its last remnant of nutrition, just drawing a line at a polystyrene McDonald's bun. Imagine if the Brighton constabulary could harness the seagulls as the French do their concierges. From chimney pot duty, they would cast a beady eye over the straggling ne'er do wells on the London Road, bristling with crutches and rabid dogs. At the first sound of a shattered beer bottle they would launch into a scorched earth swoop, driving the rabble into the nearest hostel, begging for a floor to scrub and swearing life-long temperance.

\*\*\*

Once more in search of work. I have become accustomed to the protocol. The candidates congregate in their finery, irrepressibly companionable, although each wants the other dead. Then the tour begins and the ritual of holding open the door, an act of selfless kindness that is repeated a thousand times in recognition of the iron law of Fire Regulations- nature demands a vacuum. Innate wickedness and a refusal to conform allows me to let a door snap shut, and move casually on from the scene. One candidate down. Then there's always someone too ardently keen, nodding and smiling relentlessly at every comment from the guide. And another whose anxiety gushes out in a stream of inane babble. Alas, that still leaves a preponderance of polished, confident types, who are bound to shine more than a shabby old Mule.

Each interview opens a curtain on a world of unspectacular routine, and when the cursory rejection arrives, there is no great sense of loss. Far better to cycle free as a bird over The Downs, mind cleansed by the wind and the boundless beauty. Every now and then a retreating glacier or alien spacecraft, has shaped a great looping swirl of hillside, descending in harmonious contours, peopled with contented cattle. Encounters with humans are wonderfully rare. A pair of horsey women in headscarves, bounding along with their hounds, unleash a volley of 'Mornings!' capable of serrating an eardrum. The odd professional walker rigged out in rhino boots and iron mesh socks, measures the lie of the land through the curve of his biblical crook, consults a sun dial and ploughs on through the fields like an ice cap explorer. On Sundays the walkers gather to lay claim to their birthright, and an enterprising farmer's wife cooks bacon butties in a hollow near Ditchling Beacon. One day I sat there and tuned into a huddle of farming types absorbed in serious sheep talk.

'I came across old Elsie for the first time in ages, and you know I could hardly recognise her.'

'And that black-faced beggar, hasn't she changed!'

A sullen youth sucking a straw on a gate muttered,

'Always bleating something about having a headache.'

A few silent glances were exchanged, dissolving into the grass. I resisted the temptation of a crack about woolly condoms. Better to escape the scene both tyres intact.

Carried on to Mount Harry and stood possessed by the view. A great sweep of hills woven with poppies and rape, falling away to a sparkling wall of sea. Turned around, eyes reaching across a vast plain of fields to the hazy outline of the North Downs. Descended the steep ridge to Offham, over the railway crossing, the stillness broken seconds later by a train torpedoing past. On to Barcombe, a silent cluster of country houses where even the lichened roofs look landscaped.

Strange signs of life behind the 12th century church, shovelfuls of earth being tossed into the air, panting young voices rising from a trench. A university archaeological dig. The leading lady took me in hand and gave forth as if I was a visiting professor. The significance of a stretch of clay within the chalk, the bone of a long arm, 'ridiculously long really', and a group of child skeletons. It seems the church had ordered the survey prior to building an extension. Must be the only church of the realm that is expanding its activity, but perhaps in scrunching gravel drive land, attendance at an historic pew offers a sense of security. Until, that is, the owner of the long arm manifests disquiet at being disturbed.

\*\*\*

The weather turns, wings are shackled, and the comfortable world of work takes on an enviable dimension, close enough to touch yet firmly out of bounds. How can you be qualified and yet without work in a time of full employment? Inside your head and the heads of others, something must be wrong. Weeks can pass between dispatching a C.V. and receiving the summons to attend. This hiatus in time can be the source of some confusion. Today I set off for the Marina, thinking I would be quizzed for the post of nutritionist at a keep-fit centre, when actually I was up for head chef. Realisation dawned that the interviewer was not at all conversant with glycogen stores and complex carbohydrate. I deftly conducted a soft shoe shuffle, refocused on the job in hand, and began to feel quite chipper. I could get used to this life as a chameleon job seeker. Dress up in morning suit and white bow tie, stride into the interview talking room rates and chandeliers, and emerge the newly anointed general manager of The Grand, free to indulge the top floor suite in my every sexual desire. Bring on the peanut butter. Anyway, all that chipperness disappeared on entering the kitchen. You, the paying public, have no desire to push open that swing door to Hell, and why should you, out for an evening's respite from the turmoil of your lives. Believe me; little has changed in a kitchen these past 100 years. From a room the size of a garden shed, chefs are expected to serve up wedding banquets, the stove primed like a nuclear reactor, air extractor knackered, a wall of fridges whirring and pleading in distress. An endless stream of youths enter willingly into a world turned brown by the fat fryer and centuries of grease. Catering must be the only profession where the job advert carries no mention of a wage. 'And what do you think you're worth?' they ask tight-faced, mentally conjuring a figure in shillings and pence. Euphemistic reference to the flexible working day, means split shifts and a weekend off in 2010. Walked outside, inhaled the sea air and uncoupled the last link to my kitchen career. I now want a kinder version of life. Swung a leg over my bike and realised that I had strode through the interview, trousers tucked inside my socks.

Thursday is jobs' day in 'The Argus'. When I had a seafront restaurant it used to be delivered courtesy of a genial old Pole called Stan. He began each morning polishing the brass knobs at the Theatre Royal, before waddling off on his eternal paper round. Stan would appear even when the waves were curling up on a heaving lunar tide, his trademark 'Argus!' cry, rising and ebbing away to a sigh. Dear old Argus, butt of so many comedy nights. I mean, what is an Argus and why? Out of choice I prefer the R. Goose inflection, sharing a sense of fun with R. Soles the shoe shop in Gardener Street. Both shop and Stan now sadly gone.

***

# A Happy Camel

You can hit a duff run at the Duke of York, one turgid art house movie following another, but all is forgiven when they deliver a little gem. 'The Weeping Camel' traces the nomadic life of herdsmen on the fringes of the Gobi desert. A long painful labour estranges a camel from her newborn colt, unfed and unprotected as the sandstorm blows. The shepherds conjure up a musician whose doleful sawing on a cello, allows the beast to purge its grief and be reconciled with its babie. Not big on excitement, but when the doe-eyed beauty nuzzles up to the udder, there's not a dry camel eye in the house. Imagine my surprise when cycling from Glynde; I discover a field of alluring creatures, camels without the hump. Atlantic Alpacas, darkest brown to snowy white, long looping necks nosing an interest at my approach. And there in a paddock, the authentic camel with a double hump, stretching into a tree for a spot of leafy lunch. Bleary eyed and slightly slavering, a smile of contentment all over its face.

Then up through a wood shafted with sunlight, a lost chalk quarry colonised by trees, game birds breaking cover in a shock of squawk and feather, startling the silence and peace. Climb on up above the coolie-hatted opera house, cresting above hills formed into a nest, cows congregating down in the hollow, savouring a trough of Harveys Best.

Circled round Ringmer and on to Bentley Wildfowl Park, home to the English Wine Festival. In return for a tenner they present you with a carrier bag and an empty glass. Something of an unequal exchange, the Bacchus equivalent of getting underwear for Christmas. But assume the confidence of a Bentley peacock and the balance may shift in your favour. Strode across a lawn of faded summer jackets and panama hats, into the magnificent country house where an educated tasting session was about to begin. A chinless wonder on the door muttered something about needing to buy an extra ticket, but a sharp burst of Brighton vernacular produced a more obedient response. The portcullis was raised and I settled into a sumptuous sofa, surveying the tableaux of birds in full flight.

Christopher Ann, founder of the Festival, launched into a tasting of English whites. First we inspected the colour, somewhere between corn and straw, then we agitated the liquid and perused the glass with our beaks. Now for the tasting, a little sip to start to establish the lie of the land, then a great chomping guzzle irrigating the teeth. Christopher Ann was a splendid guide, maintaining a knowledgeable commentary, and never afraid to say if a wine was just plain ordinary. Stalwart fellow that he is, he had further tastings to conduct that day on English rosés and reds.

Made for the main event in a huge L-shaped marquee, and imbibed from every vineyard and every variation of grape. Tottered out into the sunlight for a spot of Bar B Q'd lunch. Another ripe turn of phrase produced a golden firehose of a Cumberland sausage in preference to the original charred chipolata. I wolfed it down with an excellent glass of Breaky Bottom bubbly, and unfurled on the grass, watching out of the corner of my eye as a white crested pheasant strutted imperiously past. We are the masters now.

\*\*\*

Last night woken by a mosquito dive bomber. Never known this before in Brighton, but one malarial mite must have secreted itself on board the ferry, et voilà, the plague is upon us. In France you could plug a magic tablet into the mains and sleep undisturbed, windows flung wide open. No such device here, just the shock of waking under attack, flailing for the light, then prowling the bedposts with a tightly clenched Argus. And there it is, dancing on the walls like Cassius Clay, avoiding every wild swat with contemptuous ease. Not the best prelude to an interview the next day, arriving blurry eyed with an unbrushed tail. What a surreal affair. First, a serious suited type came up asking if I was Lisa. Then the long, tragic face that seemed to be in charge of affairs, silently led the way up a spiral concrete staircase. She left the questioning to Hooray Henrietta and settled into the background like a black pall of despair. Gentle Henrietta, soft voice and emollient manner, asked if I was ready to begin. Imagine if I had said no, we might still be there today. Well, in conventional fashion, I agreed to commence, and appeared to have made all the right responses until something seemed to fracture in the air. A certain brisk efficiency infected Henrietta's' voice, and at the end of proceedings El Loco offered a handshake like communion with the dead.

Intersperse the interviews with a newcomer's wide-eyed interest in the Web. Exploring university French departments as an outlet for my Normandy book, I am amazed at the ease of access, each tutor virtually throwing open the study door for a cosy tête à tête. In these times of debased intelligence, it is reassuring to learn that there are still academics who devote their lives to obscure medieval texts, or some rarefied connection between writing and sex. Mr. Forsdick, for example, specialises in 'exoticism, orality and literacy'. Puts a whole new complexion on the term 'word of mouth'. Whatever the French word for 'deed poll', bravo to Mr. Forsdick for ignoring it.

Enrolled for a little bit of learning at what was once The Tech, now reborn Brighton City College, the entrance hall and library transformed into spacious vistas of light and glass. Signed statements testify to the immaculate cleanliness of the toilet suite, but I remain dubious about the colour scheme, perilously close to penis pink. Black and white photography is appropriately located across the road in an unreconstructed monochrome set. Solid stone stairwell, worn smooth by centuries of feet, imbued with gluepot vapours from the woodwork bench. Our evening class soon establishes a familiar routine, detached from the outside world, bathed in soft red light. Each student settles into his favourite booth, adjusts the aperture, the dial marked Magenta, and projects an image onto magic paper that is gently rocked and coaxed in developer, to produce a contrast of light and shade that might rival Cartier-Bresson. Across the grainy twilight, snatches of conversation are exchanged, like dialogue with an imaginary friend. Hidden hopes cloaked in darkness, of something closer than a contact print.

Unsure how this happened really, but one stairwell along I'll be sharing an office, teaching all things cuisine. To celebrate gainful employment, I stepped out for a concert at The Dome, eyes following the sea of bows as Tchaikovsky's Fifth filled the hall, then ebbed away to that plaintive trumpet solo 'Say it'll be true love'. Conductor Kurt Masur, dispensed with baton and manuscript, and seemed something of a fraud. No beating time while absorbing whirling pages of music, just a hunched figure in a long black coat, jerking his arms like a chicken. Yet the crowd roared their approval, seduced by the image of a continental maestro in goatee white beard and tails. All is appearance, everything a charade. Henceforth I shall don pristine chef's whites and a towering toque and assume the air of Escoffier.

Brighton City College, gateway to the world. The front doors swing open and an Italian wave of sound fills the street like an exuberant cappuccino. Next a delicate flock of Chinese birds, with tender smiles and porcelain feet. Then bang, a posse of Moulescoomb girls launch the doors into orbit, bulging bare bellies giving vent to a barrage of oaths. They take up residence on the smokers' picket line alongside cocky mechanics and apprentice lads. Slipping in between, thoughtful quiet people, climbing the stairs for a spot of late life learning. There are registers scattered with double-barrelled names, the slipstream of public schools, surely all at sea in this wheeling, whirring jagged place with no discernible house rules. Yet we all somehow subsist together, the lame and the laggards, the spotty chefs and the willowy artists, hiding their talent behind a curtain of hair. The whole simmering palace of learning, kept in check by a Dads' Army of caretakers and benign security guards.

The main College building, seven storeys high, symbolises a brave attempt to transcend its humble location. Rooted deep in the wasteland of the London Road – deserted shell of a Department store and an onslaught of raging buggies – it rises up over the Bohemian splendour of The North Laines. Clothing boutiques filled with maverick gowns and sumptuous feather boas. Pubs that bake their own bread, local artists blowing glass and a café balcony from where to watch the Brighton pageant unfold. It's all gone a bit ephemeral, with greengrocers lost to scented candle land, but crafting hats and singing chimes must be better than stoking friers on the London Road.

Many moons ago when I worked with wayward children, we would take them to a deserted hilltop, and let them run wild round the windmill. They returned home exhilarated, the minibus rocking with song. Now in an age stifled by fear, I must undergo four hours of minibus 'theory', before taking the students on a trip. The first session analysed a horrific accident ending in a fireball of destruction. Suitably cowered by the impact of one foolish carefree moment, the instructor proceeded to identify the myriad dangers that await the minibus driver. 'Where is the most common place for an accident to occur?'

'A corkscrew Highland track steeped in black ice?'
'No.'
'The crumbling precipice above the quarry at Shoreham?'
'Nope.'
His eyes paraded the row of faces in front of him, until

the tension could no longer be sustained.

'The car park where the minibus is kept.' Deep exhalations of wonderment and awe. He had us captive now. Another question followed.

'What is the most dangerous item to stow on board the vehicle?' Note we had moved on from layman's 'minibus' to police parlance 'vehicle'.

'A roaring chestnut brazier?'

'No.'

'A rabid pit bull terrier?'

'Nope.'

'A black shiny bomb with hissing fuse?' The instructor dismissed my last contribution with a look of amused contempt.

'A golfing umbrella.' Renewed chorus of disbelief. 'One sharp foot on the brakes, and the umbrella launches through the bus like a javelin.' The graphic visual accompaniment brooked no argument. We were held spellbound, in thrall to a sage of vehicle safety.

\*\*\*

# The Royal Pavilion

The first Sunday in November is Old Crocks' Race. The open-topped cars roll into town, brass lamps gleaming, horns honking, bumper wicker hampers lashed to the back. The riders, battened down in outlandish mufflers and Biggles hats, proceed along the Old Steine like a Pathé newsreel of the upper classes. Stiff, cold and clinically mad. They trundle past the Old Steine Buildings which once housed civic weddings on the ground floor, and the Clapp Clinic above. One hazy memory of emerging from an appointment through a shower of confetti.

Outside, the slanting winter sun settles on the waves in a soft, luminous shimmer, silhouetting the fairground rides at the end of the Palace Pier. The clockwork climb up the Big Dipper stalls briefly in a bubble of time, before crashing into oblivion. Underneath the Arches, I catch sight of Fishwife Carol climbing into her freezer. Woman of strange habits. Sid, cross-legged looking out to sea, beak moving this way and that like a contemplative seagull. And Alan, standing sentry by the shellfish barrow, custodian of Brighton's fishing past. The air wilts around a cauldron of steaming whelks, an aroma like no other. Bottled and stored it would guarantee an end to wars of attrition. Brave captains, who had survived boiling oil and mustard gas, would desert in droves when exposed to essence of cooked whelk. Bedraggled ranks of shell-shocked troops seeking refuge inside a freezer.

The tourists gone, Brightonians reclaim their link with the sea, ambling along the lower promenade and gambolling on the beach. The heady summer cocktail of sun, booze and naked flesh, fades to a softer appreciation of the primal forces at work. A serene expanse of blue-grey, tilting gently towards the horizon, calms the space inside your head. And a wild sea, sucking and seething at the raging shingle, draws the pain from a love-torn heart.

We refuse to give up on the West Pier, nurturing the hope of something fantastic emerging from the past. Now battered and burnt into submission, the remnant closest to the shore hangs above the waves like a crushed wood lice. With each new assault from the sea, crowds gather in silent witness to the penultimate episode of a class act. The rusting ironwork of the old Ballroom is all that is left standing, defiantly presenting its profile to the setting sun. Darkness brings the seafront nightclubs to life, black-clad bouncers flexing their necks and policing the ritual queue for the door. Sound systems strike up, and soon the entire stretch of ancient arches are pulsating along the beach, drawing willowy hoods and baggy trousers, tight tight tops and stiletto feet, into the warm, charged, dark caverns: the subterranean Brighton beat!

When I had a seafront café, I used to stretch out in the back of the arch every afternoon, soothed by the cool, dark, brick dome that wrapped itself around me. Sometimes there was knocking beyond the end wall, like semaphore from a neighbouring dungeon. Signs of life in the basement of the

Old Ship Hotel. Wagons of soiled linen trundling along corridors bathed in nicotined light. Kitchen porters, arms deep in tepid brown water. Chefs frying in oil, stirring cauldrons, sparring with oven trays. Kitchen life reflecting that human pyramid at the circus, tottering yet somehow intact, the chef de partie on the commis' back, the sous chef on top of him, and finally the head chef, occasionally emerging above ground in a tall white toque, to ceremonially carve a roast or undress the salmon. The banqueting manager muttering into his moustache, 'What's that smelly oik doing here?', then casting an eye over his international brigade of waiting staff, black and white, waistcoat and bow tie, invisibly carrying salvers around tables of corporate largesse.

Antonin Carême, the father of modern cuisine, served the Prince Regent at the Royal Pavilion almost two hundred years ago. Not one to tolerate the humdrum. 'The chef who is a creature of routine; his life drips away in mediocrity.'

The kitchen was a wonder of technology, heat from the chimneys harnessed to turn the roasting spits, liberating dogs and small boys to happier times on the beach. It has been preserved in time along with Carême's festive menus, landscapes sculpted from marzipan, the Pyramids spun from sugar. Proceed through to the dining room, where the table is laid with porcelain and gold, illuminated by a chandelier more extravagant than Vienna or Versailles. Outside into the gardens, an unfussy landscape bursting with scent, the special Sultan rooftop caught in the eye of a little oval pond. The Pavilion profile never fails to impress, whether glanced from the top of a 49 bus, or caught in the amber nocturnal glow. It has survived the contempt of Victoria, the wrath of the fire bomber and the hurricane. The enduring symbol of a town that refuses to conform.

\*\*\*

My habitual Rouen resting place in the shadow of the Dungeon, is no more. Allowed myself a little luxury at L'Hôtel de la Cathédrale. Sumptuous breakfast in a salon supported by ancient Norman beams, with coach lamps hanging from anchors and cherubs brandishing torches. Each table tuned into the neighbouring tinkle of coffee cups. One night, after Monsieur Concombre had led us to the Clipper Bar, O'Kallaghans, L'Insolite and back again, Mathilde was no longer fit for the road, so I did the seminal French thing and smuggled a woman up to my bedroom. Brazenly displaying her at breakfast the next day, I must confess to a frisson of delight.

The hotel offers a sense of genteel idiosyncrasy, like sitting in front of a Monet canvas on a pot that refuses to flush. The walls are a mirage. One night I was privy to a diatribe between an angry American actress and her lapdog of a man. She unleashed her bile in a rising crescendo of 'Aye', I the victim, I the disrespected, I who married that schmuck. The poor old critter finally made a bolt for the door, only to be felled by an admonishment like rolling thunder. Hard to imagine the hunched, grey figure at the breakfast table, the object of such venomous desire.

The 'Fields of Vision' exhibition at the Musée des Beaux Arts was a happy surprise. One door opening onto a catwalk over warm dark water, a firmament of lights projecting your image a thousand times onto the mirrored walls of a magic womb. If I were still resident in Rouen, I would return each day to walk upon the water in more appropriate attire. A pink flamingo, a dervish whirling in a sea of silk scarves. Le Petit Prince floating serenely through the stars.

\*\*\*

The environs of the Mulehouse were once so non-descript, the Electric Board insisted the road did not exist. Gradually, with the encroachment of London's nouveau riche, the area has taken on a more townhouse look, with shiny red sports cars cosying up to the kerbside, and loft extensions cluttering the street. Now, from being a no man's land somewhere between the Lewes Road and the railway tracks, we are re-born the 'Roundhill' district. Desperate for an identity, the new breed has unearthed a past when wheat was ground at the communal mill amid a frenzy of Maypole dancing. Barely a week goes by without the consecration of a special tree, or an exhibition of sepia prints. Mercifully, the area has not been totally disinfected. The ramshackle building opposite remains home to a warren of flats, which on hot summer nights open their windows on spectacular domestic disputes. Last week, while in the uncompromising embrace of the dental hygienist, I became privy to the innermost workings of that house. She had, it seems, once lived there, and she portrayed a Boswellian picture of drunken violence and mysterious disappearance. One day the bailiffs planted a notice on an empty flat, announcing that all the residents' chattels had been removed. 'Do you think he had it done on the NHS?' I asked.

Unwise to utter those three initials to a dental hygienist, especially when prone in a helpless state. Her picking and polishing came under exclusively 'Private' jurisdiction. I gingerly passed my tongue over seeping, damaged gums, while she expounded on the wonders of a new flossing device.

'You can even use it while driving the car,' she said.
'I've got a bike.'
'Absolutely no problem.'
You can just see the headline in The Argus:
'Cyclist bites dust while flossing teeth.'

\*\*\*

The Level is a flat segment of urban grass, surrounded by angry traffic. Lines of trees stand awkward and distressed, dreaming of crystalline air and birdsong. In December it is just an empty space you cross on the long trudge home, but when spring arrives the Level comes alive with tactical five-a-side, dogs barking at boules and flaming torches twirling through the night. Tall hedges enclose the skateboard ramp, where boys watch intently, occasionally launching up and down, like hamsters on a wheel. Across the road, the old Municipal College has been turned into luxury flats, two columns of chimneys buffed to an earthy pink. They once warmed hands in a technical drawing class, but now offer the comfort of an empty hearth. One municipal building dead, another re-born.

This month the new library facade was unveiled, reflecting the turbans and minarets of the Corn Exchange against a changing canvas of clouds. Inside, everything is light and green, pillars that seem hardly to exist, sofas in the sky, a vast space lit by the sun and human thoughts. The first weekend, it seemed that half of Brighton were there, staking out the plaza, pacing the walkways, marvelling at this gem of civic pride. A sense of bewilderment among those gentle folk for whom the old library was once home, perplexed at the novelty of it all and those lost corners of silence. Perhaps they will find refuge in Hove.

A new cliché has been honed, 'Hove is like Brighton of old, before it got trendy.' I'm not convinced by this homily to Hove, but one fine embodiment of the past deserves preservation. Up towards Blatchington Mill, the Engineerium sits on the site of the old water pumping station, and harbours a history of mechanical endeavour. Ornately gilded mangles, the world's smallest motor coach, an impeccable motorbike with curvaceous burgundy sidecar. Steam takes centre stage in the form of the 'Goldstone Giant', a magnificent commotion of wheels and pistons, working relentlessly with power and grace. Men with oily cloths and attentive faces keep the behemoth beauty in pristine shape. A sign on their glass-panelled workshop paints a portrait of an endangered species, the mechanical engineer.

The Goldstone Ground might not have known giants of the footballing scene, but less than 20 years ago it resounded to crowds of 30,000, and was a whisker from winning the Cup. Today the Seagulls have no ground, no money and all hope of building a new home has foundered on the buffers of planning consent. The faithful file into the Withdean stadium with all the animation of a wake, Argus billboards exhorting them to 'Make a Noise' and 'Keep The Faith'. The Albion footballing tradition, in danger of becoming a museum piece.

***

St. James Street – gateway to Kemptown, with more gays per square inch than dresses in a Cardinal's cupboard. The cavalcade of queens up and down the hill is pure performance art, eyes rotating fantastically with that unique gay ability to track a guy directly behind his head. The Pink Pamper, Bona Foodie, Dorothy's Drag Emporium; shop signs lifted from a 'Round the Horn' script. Sometimes it is all a bit intense, the heavy leather torpor of the Bulldog bar, or the can-can of 'folles' heading down to the club. Better when casually intertwined into the rich tableau of Kemptown life. Business types pacing, brash kids skating, pensioners waiting for the eternal bus. The 'Golden Girl' eaterie with Windsor Castle place mats, and 'The Laughing Onion' with a singing chef. The barber's chair under a brooding portrait of Henry the Eighth, and 'Doggy Fashion', window onto the world of canine coiffure. Indulgence is the coming thing. Tacky B&B's with dodgy mattress and rubber sheets are re-born as 'hotel boutique'. The Piccasso room or the Dali suite, with trays of golden brioche and bathtubs drawn from asses' milk. Designer emporia have sprung up in search of the nouveau elite, but better to search the Flea Market for the outlandishly unique.

***

# Festival nights

His great, great, great, grand pappy started making wine in 1829. 'And now,' says Genaro de Cala, Duque de Diano, 'it is my turn.' He has brought the fruits of his Spanish cellar to a tiny shop opposite the Corn Exchange where you can eat paella, chew chorizo, and learn how sherry vinegar matures for a hundred years. The Slow Food Movement writ large. Genaro offers tastings of everything authentic from olive and grape, breaking into a sunlit smile whenever his English falls into place. I popped in for a spot of tapas before a night out at The Spiegel Tent, hottest venue at this year's Festival. A burlesque combination of sex and circus, like The Blue Angel on a trapeze. Light filters through stained glass windows, onto panels of mirrors reflecting the audience in their cosy compartments, eyes transfixed on the bizarre parade. Two bleached boys glide up the tent pole, and back-flip dramatically into a kettle drum of waves. A cabaret chanteuse in latticed bodice, coaxes her voice across smoking coals and dominates the stage. Then a gyrating presence in pink PVC, salamis a cucumber, unhinges her mouth and swiftly devours her sword. Up steps fraulein all in black, apart from a little red hanky. A sequence unfolds of the handkerchief disappearing inside her fist, then emerging in an item of clothing, that is casually tossed away. Cut to the hanky surfacing in her last remaining garment, a skimpy black panty, sensationally discarded to uproarious applause. Still one more scene to the trick, the hanky lost in the fist, then re-emerging scarlet-faced, from an unholy bodily crevice. Cue collapse of Spiegel Tent.

A lot of Festival spectacular is free and out of doors. One windswept day, I looked out of my seafront café to discover a dance of the butterflies, specially choreographed for an audience of one. Another time, drawn to the sea on a wave of sun, the whole of Brighton cascaded down the Colonnade in a fiesta of samba. No such scenes on The Level last night. A Gallic street theatre performed a tortuous set on the meaning of time, then a fire engine appeared, filled with shouting clowns. The terms 'German' and 'comic' should really have sounded the alarm. Unexpectedly rewarded today by a tight rope walker, bobbing about the saintly faces on the wall of the Chapel Royal, casually playing a violin. His cheeky minstrel hat stealing the show.

With the Festival, the town opens its doors like blossoming buds of May. Neighbours play host to exhibitions of art, and corners of local heritage emerge from the dark. I must have walked down Middle Street a hundred times, unaware of the gem of Victorian architecture that lies behind the synagogue walls. Two lines of arches proceed towards the tabernacle of scrolls, the whole interior bathed in natural light. Every window a beautiful mosaic of coloured glass, and upstairs in the ladies' gallery, gleaming brass balustrades and marble pillars rising above the Ark. A couple of young men keep the faith alive, but the rest are physically rooted in the past. One describes how this was the first synagogue fitted with electricity, and you could almost see him there as a child, blinking up at the yellow light. Another unfolds the mystery of the little Jewish cemetery tucked away on the Ditchling Road. It contains the tomb of Henry Solomon, chief constable of Brighton, killed by a carpet thief in 1844. You can visit the scene of the crime in the dungeon of the Town Hall, where in a frenzied attack; John Lawrence grabbed a poker and delivered the terrible blow. The Chief's cocked hat offered scant protection, and he was dead the next day. Every manner of police attire is on display, jackets lined and jackets old, truncheons as long as your leg, and the traditional white helmet that once patrolled along the Prom. A century of miscreants inscribed on thick cell walls, 'Dave the Rocker', 8th June 1964.

Set off slightly dubious for the tour of Brighton station. Imagined a group of autistic men with mis-shapen clothes and faces, duffel bags with flasks of tea and pickled egg packed lunches. In the event, all apprehension unfounded, not an anorak in sight. The history of the place is almost epic. Six thousand navvies built the first line to Shoreham, and the viaduct to Lewes comprised twenty seven arches and ten million bricks. Horse drawn cabs ran to and from the station, and there was even a Horse Hospital to soothe a weary hoof. The punishing climb up Trafalgar Street was too much for old Dobbin, so a gentler tunnel was navigated, emerging beside the rails. One subterranean stretch has long been home to the station Rifle Club. Generations of commuters who have rolled the rock of Sisyphus up Trafalgar Street, searched in vain for a train, sunk to their knees, pounded the platform and inveighed into the steel and glass heavens that 'British Rail/

Connex/ Southern want shooting!', may never know how close they came to the truth.

Final Festival outing to Wild Park, a sweeping hollow in the hills just outside of town. A procession of wayward Spanish trumpets driven along by drums, wound its way past the striking image of a woman, half wide-eyed Thatcher in trilby hat and tie, half the floral costume of Freda Karlo. The musicians and their entourage settled around an enormous edifice, like Cruella Deville's mountain top retreat. Torch bearers knelt to ignite the touch paper, engulfing Casa Cruella in a ring of cackling flame. A huge pall of smoke swayed in the sky, like the day the West Pier died, the inferno eventually fading to a shell of bare bones. Just when you were wondering if this was the end of the affair, a battery of guns exploded from the hills, fireworks shattering the sky, drawing forth a chorus of hounds from the Crusty encampment in the trees. Streamers soared from the hillside, imploding in a cascade of stars, and the roar of the crowd brought forth renewed volleys of shellfire, each more exuberant than the last. On and on it went, faces shining in delight, the hollow brimming with excitement in the light of a luminous moon.

\*\*\*

In most organisations, meetings are dread events where administrative clones exact revenge for the barrenness of their lives. Time freezes over as the entrails of the last meeting are exhumed, points of order raised, and the 'team' transforms into Sartre's depiction of man as an inert, lifeless object, like the gnarled root of a tree. Not so the chef lecturers' meeting at City College Brighton. Eight o'clock on a Friday morning, each entrant infuses a pot of coffee to erase the excesses of the night before, then launches into a round of raucous banter, during which the business somehow gets done. Richard the pastry chef, sole survivor of the culling of the Old Guard, offers a more cerebral contribution, suggesting 'Rott Filer' as the dog routinely blamed for eating a student's work.

At a recent meeting of the whole Department, the college Principal was billed to attend. Her reputation burnished by the plethora of lieutenants that occupy the fifth floor, it was the first time I had actually clapped eyes on our leader. She displayed a no-nonsense approach to business, settling back in her chair in string vest and cigar. Apparently new legislation has been enacted concerning intimate contact in the classroom. From now on, pastoral care will have to be conducted in a pair of rubber gloves. All this delving into the nether regions turned the room strangely still. Several hands reached for the mineral water and deep comfort glugging. Strange how the water bottle has assumed an essential role in the modern meeting; sleek computer, personal phone and an Evian. Slick suited bombast, in constant need of irrigation.

Nothing could prepare me for the day long 'validation meeting', when a panel of university worthies chewed over every detail of the teaching programme. These are desperately arid people, physically incapable of making a simple statement, twisting interminably around the vexed question of whether to 'analyse' or 'evaluate' a student's work. At one stage the chief Honcho drawled out a question, so incoherently dull that the assemblage froze in a state of academic rigor mortis, the spell broken only by the crashing entrance of the coffee trolley. After the break, surfing on a buzz of caffeine, a surprisingly succinct question was asked. Given the small size of the teaching team, what would happen if one member dropped out to have a baby? Our genial head of department gathered his thoughts inside his throat, before replying that we would all rally round to fill the breach. This stray shaft of humour unshackled an enormous sense of relief; the business was swiftly concluded and we all made for the pub in a strange parody of normal life.

\*\*\*

The Chattri moves deceptively about The Downs. The first time I approached its little domed roof, it retreated into the distance, until lost inside a nettle tunnel, I turned tail and trotted home. A second attempt was foiled by mist lying low over autumnal fields. Third time round, I changed tack, crossing the pedestrian bridge near Patcham, and unbolting the gate on a little sanctuary commanding Brighton and the sea. During the First World War, the Royal Pavilion was converted into a hospital for Indian soldiers. Stories are told of men recovering consciousness, believing they had arrived in Paradise. Those who died of their wounds were cremated at The Chattri, a white marble monument surrounded by stunted trees. The enclosure was filled with birdsong and the remorseless howling of a cow. A neighbouring field shone lavender blue, the hedgerow ablaze with poppies. That night a storm gathered over Brighton; first inconsequential, like furniture being moved upstairs, then crashing through the sky in a torrent of rain. I wondered how the Chattri fared that night, turbans flying on horseback, Ghurkhas dancing with glinting blades, challenging the storm to a duel. Or watching serenely, a sentry above the city.

***

# Heritage Sussex

There is a grand heritage of photography in Brighton. In 1897 Alfred Darling beavered away in his bedroom at 47 Chester Street, designing equipment for the film pioneers William Friese Greene and Arthur Albert Esmé Collings. Men with telescopic names. 'Mad Jack' Bennett Stanford, one of the family that owned Preston Manor, was the first reporter to film action from the front line in the Boer War. George Albert Smith started out as a stage hypnotist, then transformed St. Anne's Well Gardens into a pleasure park with magic lantern shows. In 1909 he invented Kinemacolour, the earliest form of motion pictures produced on coloured film.

The Duke of York was the first cinema, followed by The Regent at the Clock Tower, 'a gorgeous temple of the silent drama,' which held three thousand people. Today, the 'Dukies' enjoys a renewed lease of life but otherwise there are only two concrete bunkers to watch a film, the multiplex at The Marina and The Odeon on the Kings Road. The dearth of picture houses has not diminished enthusiasm for photography. The streets abound with amateur enthusiasts capturing punk peacocks, pensive seagulls, chimney pots clambering over the hills. A few years ago there was a terrific exhibition by Mark Power, depicting all the locations from

'The Shipping Forecast': Cromarty, Rockall, German Bite, landscapes on the edge of the world.

The town museum throws up diverse images of Brighton life. A surreal pink sofa in the shape of Mae West's lips. A couple of fishermen splicing rope beneath thick woolly hats. The history of Brighton Boozers from smugglers arms to stark bars, cold and dark with menace. Pubs look more comfortable now, with real food and ales amid a warm and cosy hubbub. 'The Park Crescent' has grainy prints on the wall commemorating times past; the Chain Pier, trams in the street, a grandstand finish at the races. Street scenes of baggy caps and long skirts, and a dog staring straight at the camera.

\*\*\*

The Volks Railway rattles along under The Colonnade, drawing to a halt at a stark little platform just out of sight of the nudist beach. Opposite is Black Rock, where generations of homosexual men have ended the night stalking 'The Bushes'. The ritual circuit of Kemptown pubs, and the sticky stairwells of 'Revenge', fail to turn up life's young dream, and the procession continues to Black Rock where anything can emerge from the bushes; Captain Hook, The Village People, bank managers bristling with chains. There is talk of transforming the place into an ice rink, the whole gay merry-go-round swirling by in a parade of spangled waistcoats and articulated buttocks, coloured hankies flagging every sexual peccadillo. Contestants nervously awaiting the judges' verdict; straight zeroes for technical merit but 'cinq points' for artistic flair.

This summer, Dutch sculptors created a city of sand on the wasteland beyond Black Rock. Pharaohs and the pyramids projecting striking shadows onto the graffiti-strewn cladding of the Marina walls. Graffiti improves the Marina. Volcanic eruption, a plague of jellyfish, anything would improve the Marina. It is only worth crossing to reach the new undercliff path to Saltdean. The tide pulls out to reveal vast stretches of lava rock, boulders draped in dark brown seaweed like wet Rastafarian hair. Days of innocent pleasure spent fishing with rod and net. Usually the path is promenaded by brisk retirees, but this morning Ovingdean beach was winding down after an all night rave. I have never seen people so staggeringly exhausted, just one raver still able to waft a hippy hand in the air. The request for a light borne on a blast of bad breath that would have stripped a rock of limpets. A couple of regular walkers stared at the intruders, contempt and defiance mushrooming behind impenetrable shades. Their dogs growled and scratched in the dirt, then beat an honourable retreat.

The swimming pool at Saltdean has been restored to its original Art Deco splendour, but the Grand Ocean Hotel stands silent and forlorn. Constructed on a wave of optimism before the war, it slipped from luxurious panache to Butlin's mode and now languishes behind barbed wire. 'Shadow Security' patrols the grounds, an aphorism of our times. I continued over Telescombe Cliffs but got lost in search of Breaky Bottom vineyard. The Ridgeview Estate is easier to find, sheltering under a headland of the Downs just north of Ditchling. They produce quite stunning 'champagne' wines. During early Spring, fires are lit along the rows of vines to dispel the threat of frost. The view from the Downs of a flaming vineyard, must be something to savour at night.

The pinot noir grapes used for this champagne come from the 'Hidden Spring Vineyard'. For eighteen years they produced a range of wines in the thriving little village of Horam, but they no longer find wine viable, and now just grow the grapes. The day I popped in for a tasting, the roof was being ripped off the wine shop, neatly stripping the occasion of any pretension. Normally I am unable to find the words to describe a taste sensation. No problem here though, the 'Hidden Spring' red is positively smoky; two thousand taste buds humming with delight. Get down to Horam while stocks last, then drop a line to the Chancellor, commanding a measure of respect for our plucky English winemakers.

\*\*\*

Last weekend I found myself in Rouen for a 'son et lumière spectacle'; an interpretation of Monet on the cathedral walls. Light was projected from the window where Monet once stood, first highlighting the Gothic darkness of the place, then the lines of masonry and finally the dappled blobs we know as Impressionist art. Another shift in focus recreated the facade as an artist's palette, with a great splurge of blood on the cathedral doors. After that, the projections seemed to lose their way, and the discordant urban soundtrack had a dispiriting effect. I stayed with the crowd for a second sequence, eyes tilted upwards, trying to fathom a higher meaning.

I once flew over the cathedral in a little Cettna plane,

flirting with the bell towers and the dockyard cranes. Then we coasted over countryside, and followed the wake of the ferry across the sea. Left at Beachy Head, the view took on a new familiarity, the piers shifting in and out of focus through ephemeral wisps of cloud. Rising anxiety as we descended to Shoreham airport, bounced onto the runway, then taxied benignly, exultant and alive. Jumped out of the cockpit, through the art deco doors into a lounge furnished like a smart Parisian café.

The walls chart the history of the place. Opened in 1910 by Howard Pifford, onetime music hall performer, who flew the legendary 'Humming Bird'. 1936 must have been a halcyon year, people hanging from the balconies to watch the summer show. Inside, a demure barman in white jacket and tie, flanked by soda siphons and polished glass. How many of his pilots returned from the war? On August the 19th 1942, an attempt was made to land Allied troops at Dieppe. You have only to walk the precipitous heights either side of Dieppe to know the assault was doomed. German fortifications are still embedded in the cliffs today. One hundred RAF planes failed to return, the worst single loss of the war. Of the two squadrons that flew from Shoreham, six planes were shot down over the sea, one crashed at Friston, another on Littlehampton beach. Only two made it back to base, damaged but safe. Many artefacts of the war can be found in the airport archive; a German bomb, an ejector seat, a brown leather pilot's cap on a delicate glass face.

Shoreham beach is a tranquil place. A great sweep of pebbles corralled into sheltered havens, a line of beach huts patrolling the sea. A little way along, the river estuary is filled with house boats, brightly coloured and eccentrically shaped, the authentic Brighton marina. Each mooring displays original traits. Mauve artichokes thistles flowering in an old bath tub. Antique carpets hanging out to air and lots of bold artwork. A notice explains how one house served as a torpedo boat during the war. The wording has been scorched by the sun, but you can just make out the name of the craft, 'Spitfire of the Sea'. Up above, a tiny aircraft trundles over Lancing College, and disappears into the sky.

\*\*\*

And Billy is almost free. Seeing him again has done strange things to me. Limbs normally quick and efficient are leaden with fatigue. Nights of semi-wakefulness, re-visiting the stations of our past. One weekend awakened by ringing bells. Best to ignore the stranger at the darkened door. Bells keep ringing and determined hands shake the bars of the garden gate. I throw open the window and there he is, fled the confines of that cold place, stomping his hoof on the step. An outlawed, whirlwind night, intense, anxious and fun, snatched from the guardians of the state. Billy Mule, mourned these past eight years, is back inside my life.

They didn't take too kindly to his escapade, but the dust settled and now Billy is busy gardening just twenty miles away. A chance to explore the countryside thereabouts. The 'Cuckoo Trail' skirts 'The Dinkum' pub at Polegate, then travels north along a disused railway, past a former station platform that is now someone's house. Days spent pulling leavers and shunting out of the garage. Turned left into

Hellingley, an immaculate little village built around a churchyard. The proximity of homes to the gravestones removing the shadow of death. No pub or tinkling village shop, just a crescent of cosy cottages, the red tiled walls and lattice windows sloping comfortably into shape. One house stands square and double-glazed, a brazen affront to the gingerbread set. I booked into Globe Cottage, a lovely rambling place with an old dog asleep in the garden, marooned on a giant cushion. In the bedroom, no tasteless teasmade or hanging TV, just gently creaking furniture and birdsong busy at the window. Next door, a majestic bathroom with enormous sunken tub and fluffy toga to dry off in. Breakfast followed in splendid fashion, home grown eggs, tasty little sausages and four different pots of marmalade.

Early morning sun slanted through the trees of the Saxon churchyard, the grass deep in catkins. This is heritage Sussex: monasteries and castles that spread like beacons of power from the Norman landings at Pevensey Bay. Cycled through Upper Dicker, ancestral home of Frankie Howard, arriving at Michelham Priory on the banks of the river Cuckmere. Lassoed the bike to an iron penny farthing, and was immediately drawn up the twisting stone staircase of the gatehouse. Tucked into a recess at the top, a privy designed with a sense of freedom. The pot perched a mile above the meadow, turdies tumbling into space.

Out in the grounds surprise sculptures emerge from the grass. A fragile wooden bridge sways across the river, imbuing the lily leaves with carnivorous intent. Inside the building, a generous complement of middle-aged ladies discourse happily on Priory life. The Order founded by

Augustus the Hippo, the mill on the river restored to good health. One of the ladies bestrides the stool of an ornamental piano, unveiling the timbre of a magic mandolin. Then onto the medieval kitchen. A winch to raise the cauldron from raging boil to gentle simmer, and a clever piece of rigging to turn the spit. Beside the window, a bacon cupboard where the meat settled after preserving with salt and smoke. Stepped outside into the 'physic garden', and remedies for every human complaint. Broken bones, pregnancy, attacks of colic and the vapours. Searched in vain for a herbal leaf that might defuse a lifetime of flatulence.

Carried on to Arlington where the Old Oak Inn occupies the site of the former Almshouse. Precious few poor houses in evidence today, every barn and forge perfectly restored. There are stately homes at Firle and Glynde, each with a tea room filled with episodes of country life. Two blousy ladies extol the virtues of an honest hound; absolute loyalty and unconditional love. One neighbour, recently departed, requested burial alongside her dog in preference to her husband. The corpse in limbo these past two weeks while the word of the will is contested. Other tales followed filled with peril. The 'lethal' cockerel that lies in wait, capable of shredding your wellies. The gentle flock of geese, ravaged by a fox, the farmer's wife inconsolable with grief. Burial arrangements yet to be announced.

Arrived at Charleston House, home of the Bloomsbury set. The place was shut, so I poddled around the pond with statues leaning this way and that, and an ancient artist crumpled under a huge panama hat. Carried along Bo Peep Lane, which climbs an alcove in a wall of hills, like the hearth of the South Downs. From the summit, brown harvested fields disappeared into a shimmering haze. Cycling south, the river slalomed its way through Cuckmere Haven, into a fusion of sea and sky. Made my way to Berwick station where the signalman was hoovering his signal box. A little rainbow flag fluttering from the top.

\*\*\*

The coastal towns east of Brighton are stations on a line that time forgot. Places of tranquillity verging on bleakness. The train travels a glorious path in the shadow of the Downs, scatters the pebbles on Cooden Beach, then picks its way through wooded hillsides to Rye. A fast new service has just appeared, linking the Eurostar terminal at Ashford. A little two carriage affair that immediately demonstrates nippy intent by speeding round the viaduct out of Brighton, the lay lines to Preston Circus and the Racecourse turning like spokes on a wheel. Stopped briefly at Bexhill to peruse the De La Warr Pavilion, curvaceous stairway rising smoothly above the waves. An exhibition of 'Variety' in a town that has precious little. Then onto Rye, one of the famous 'cinq ports' now curiously bereft of sea. The town straddles a little hill, shops filled with treasures: 'Herald and Heart Hatters', 'Simon the Pieman' and an old brick school house that is now a record shop. This is serious eating country, pubs laid with crisp linen, incidentally selling beer. Suttons, the fish shop offering venison and wild boar as well as plump local scallops.

South of Rye, a castle built as a sea defence stands

marooned in a plain of empty dreams. Regimented caravan parks and a home for orphaned donkeys. Then it's up another hill, and through an arch flanked by pretty turrets. Winchelsea, immaculate cottages, communal well and a truly 'Little Shop'. A huge log fire lures you into the pub, with gleaming copper kettles and two copper fire hydrants. The village church possesses the grandeur of an abbey, mummies staring blankly into the twilight of coloured glass. Looking into the distance, signs for the beach appear like a mirage. But there it is, flat and featureless, hidden behind an embankment. A fragile defence against the melting ice caps. This coastline once belonged to Fécamp in Normandy, and subsequently witnessed centuries of rampaging between England and France. In 1377 the French stole the bells from St. Mary's church; the next year the English brought them back again. Gunnels filled with duty-free and barrels of Bénédictine.

***

# Seagull City

This seagull thing is hard to explain. There is no way you would cradle a seagull as you might a fragile dove. Or warm to its militant right to roam among your rubbish. One bird signals daybreak with a raucous hacking cough, then every roof takes up the cry like the chorus line on a chain gang. On cold comfort days they eyeball stray puppies and unguarded prams, spiked guttering and CCTV failing to deter their Hitchcockian intent. They launch formation bombing raids capable of targeting a bald head from a thousand feet. Once on the terrace of 'The Cook & Fiddle', a missile landed right inside a customer's glass, a sauvignon tsunami erupting in her face. Despite these unsocial habits, seagulls remain the proud symbol of our town, a swaggering affront to all authority. 'We might be skint but we've got the sea.' The mascot of a football team that flirted with the afterlife of the Vauxhall Conference League, decamped to Gillingham, then rented the Sunday Park at Withdean. This week John Prescott settled down after a triple chip buttie, jowls rippling contentedly about his face. He surveyed the acres of planning reports carpeting the office, belched emphatically and proclaimed to his minions, 'They <u>shall</u> have a stadium on Falmer hill!' Behold The Albion arisen from the ashes in a flight of blue and white seagulls.

***

Tonight in the kitchens of the Royal Pavilion, preparing a Regency banquet – pigeon pie with Madeira sauce, beetroot pancakes with asparagus. The stove, the ovens, and the salamander pump the kitchen with white heat, yet at service time the window is shut lest a rogue breathe of air cool the plates. You could almost hear the scalding voice of Carême when a pan of soup is dropped on the floor. 'Why are you so small in talent and so mean in invention?' The punishing traditions of catering persist over centuries, a sort of bravura pride in working twelve hours on the hoof in a hothouse sealed off from the outside world and the soft comfort of the dining room. Uniquely on this occasion, the brigade of student chefs are summoned front of house for a vote of thanks from the Prince Regent and his assembled guests, wigs and powdered faces shaking with applause. It is all quite overwhelming, caught in the light of the giant chandelier, then we all troop back to the kitchen to tackle a mountain of pots.

    You can see why coffee shops have taken hold; they are effortless by comparison. A little steam expended at the espresso machine, but otherwise a light-hearted menu of salad leaves, and the customer left to construct his own little space with newspaper or music machine. Free to tune in or out of the transient decor of the place. A cascade of tasselled hair bounding by on Doctor Martins, stripy leggings and a perky tartan skirt. Students nodding and rolling up, raking through the embers of a legendary night out. Tarquin the Otter and Percy Gape, posh tones peppered with 'geezer' and 'mate'. An Italian man dressed in black, with a powerful cane and a Homburg hat. Entrances, exits, a window on life, glimpsed through the eye of a coffee cup.

We have just one café on the Lewes Road, one café and a 'caring lady funeral director'. Once home to three green grocers, two post offices and a cake decorating shop, the decline of the High Street has gathered pace with whole sections of shop front now boarded up. This month even the petrol station gave up the ghost, redundant nozzles sealed off behind wire perimeter fencing. Unlikely that a garden centre will emerge on the forecourt, the fuel bunker contaminated with a cargo of toxic waste. The cold wind blowing down the high street comes from the Sainsbury's on the gyratory system, a perfect symbol of corporate blandness, bleak and inhospitable. The sun never shines on the gyratory system, exhausts pipes funnelling a cloud of despair, life caught in an eternal round of traffic and wayward shopping trolleys. Perhaps one day the old railway viaduct will be rebuilt. Motorists lifted from their cars onto a ferris wheel, then gently deposited in liveried carriages that glide through Hanover tunnel to Kemptown, where swaying palm trees usher the crowds into a people's palace, reclaimed from bingo for nights of romantic dancing. Uplifting waltzes, smouldering sambas, the tempestuous Brighton tango.

Further up the Lewes Road stands the Allen & West engineering factory that became Brighton Poly. Old Marge used to work there making submarine parts during the war. One of just two girls sent on a residential course to learn post graduate tool sharpening. Uproarious tales of a wooden leg lost in the dormitory during the blackout. Later the factory became carpet storage for Hanningtons, the department store that once graced half of North Street. Legions of staff draped in specs and measuring tapes, insulated from the outside world by bedding and goose down pillows. About ten years ago, saplings were planted in the polytechnic car park, the facade was re-rendered on a giant mortar board, and behold the University of Brighton was born, Oxbridge beside the sea.

A quarter of a mile up the hill is Moulescoomb estate, designed after the first world war as a model garden suburb. Modern folklore now knows it as bandit country, I-Pods dealt off the back of a lorry, police patrolling in helicopters. The first time I visited friends up there, the street sign was missing. The next time the whole street had disappeared. There must be something to say for an estate within striking distance of wild deer and rabbits, but then I don't live there. I live in the comfort zone on the other side of the road. Peace and comfort is the enduring impression when you finally arrive at Lewes. One immaculate bowls green within the Priory ruins, another above the castle walls. The high street is a place of wonderment, not a single chain store, just distinctive little shops. Ripe brie melting over the counter of Beckworths' Deli. Antiquarian bookshops with rows of solid covers that could prop up a little house. The whole town once turned on local hops and malt, but Harveys is now the last remaining brewery. Their special bitters commemorate milestones of local history. Tom Paine Alcohol, Armada Ale and an Elizabethan number that could blow your head off on Bonfire Night.

\*\*\*

Head inland from the seafront and Brighton is a perpendicular place. Take an uninitiated Londoner up Hanover and he will turn turtle on Southover Street, gasping for oxygen and a taxi. Brightonians perfect a plodding momentum to carry them up the hill, reflecting the philosophy of the life-long Spurs supporter; you need to travel the tunnel of darkness to appreciate glimpses of the promised land. The view from 'The Setting Sun', stretching all the way to Shoreham. The racecourse falling away in mid-circuit to the glint of chalk cliffs and a febrile sea.

Jim and Nat's house is perched on the ascent to the Seven Dials; high above the railway sheds with a view of the whole town. Jim and John played guitar and sax on the terrace of 'The Cook & Fiddle', each instrument instinctively following the pitch and flight of the other. Jim would roll up, amp strapped to his skateboard, guitar on his back, a symbol of the art school at Grand Parade. He is now deep in children and a regular job, but still finds time for band practice at New England House, home to the 'Real Patisserie' and a warren of small businesses. Hard to conceive of wholesome bread rising in such an ugly place, or melodies flowering behind the cold metallic walls. There are more auspicious settings for music in Brighton. Saint Bartholomew's stands like a great ark above the London Road. Last winter a Russian male voice choir filled the church with golden melancholy, wan clothes and faces reflecting a bygone age. Another night following a classical concert, the orchestra filed into the Harlequin club on the back street behind Woolies. Powdered transvestites displaced from the bar by a bevy of bow tie and tails.

Recently stumbled upon a performance in Sussex University. Upstairs at The Meeting House, a turret of coloured glass glowing in the winter sun. Images of urban life accompanied a cello that soared to a mosaic in the dome of the roof, that turns like a stairway to heaven. The campus is a wonderful place. The theme of slopes and arches softens the concrete and brick. A great rugby goal rises on slabs of stone, and a line of paths sweeps in and out of the Arts buildings with a powerful sense of unity. Something good is cooking on the grass outside the Slope Bar. Quinoa from the Andes, chunky garlic and orange peppers with a lime and mango pickle. An Inca bonanza for just two pounds fifty. Students saunter up to the steaming pan with a carefully nurtured look. Fringe stuck to the forehead and a sliver of bare belly. I feel like a fashion relic, forelock long departed and midriff clad against the cold. Thirty five years ago I spent weekends here, kipping on my brother's floor. Never stepped out of a pair of velvet flared denims, a scraggy old woolly and an army surplus jacket. I gaped in awe at a world with so much freedom, so much sleep and so many brands of revolution. All granted by a state like a benevolent Danish uncle. We grew up in cherished times.

\*\*\*

The sea swelling serenely on an improbably high tide. Gently rising and falling with the snoring of the Ancient Mariner, happily ensconced below decks after a satisfying feed. Every now and then a belch of post-prandial contentment sends a wave crashing over the sea wall, scattering the promenaders at Ovingdean beach. Dread to think of the impact of sudden awakening from a shipwrecked dream. Half way to the horizon, a pale spotlight of winter sun lights up a stage in aquamarine. A gathering of gulls intertwine in modern dance, hang wistfully in the air then soar in tight formation before wheeling away. The performance framed by banks of cloud that soon eclipse the stage, turning the pebbles cold and forbidding as the walls of Roedean School.

This winter 'The Shoreline' was given pride of place at the Dyke Road natural history museum. The entire catalogue of flotsam and jetsam, from sea horse fossils to toxic waste. Every branch of the gull family is represented here, casting protective glances over fledglings in a nest, or searching back to distant times unconfined by glass. Walls of birds restored to a semblance of life, with captivating names like the 'Honey Buzzard'. The whole museum is set in a quieter age, when families took their holiday for a week beside the sea, returning to the B&B each night to await the gong for dinner. Campbells soup and cotton wool bread, tired meat and soggy veg, all greeted with gentle cooing.

***

'The Zap' occupies a special place in the folklore of Brighton nightlife. 'Club Shame' on a Wednesday provided theatre of the unexpected, exotic creatures parading on an aerial catwalk, the outlandish contingent led by a man called Grace, a looping feather from his headdress once tickling my ear at the bar. Sinuous beauties performed on the podium, orchestrating the nodding mortals below. The Mules would survey from their perch on the balcony, watching the happy trance unfold, then thread their way to a favoured corner, Billy dancing with rhythmic ease.

This week 'The Zap' shut its doors, leaving a sense of loss even though I have long called time on nights of clubbing, and now enjoy more mellow pursuits. Cycling through the canopy of trees down to Stanmer Park, where 'The Wee House' in the farm museum offers the perfect setting for a quiet life. Cooking pots, an accordion, a stove and a simple bed. Should one mule stomp off in a stubborn fit of pique, the painted wagon next door would provide a perfect retreat. Later reconciled, in a lazy nuzzling of muzzles, we might reminisce about famous nights at 'The Zap' that always ended tumbling through the front door, Billy biting my leg. Laughing and falling, entwined together, we wrap ourselves in snapshots of our lives.

\*\*\*

# **BRIGHTON SEAFRONT**

**Beach sky**

**Dog in bag**

## Fisherman's Quarter

**And they're off!**

**Seagull**

# Benches

**Palace Pier**

**Curtains for fishing**

**Three generations of fishwife**

# Fishing Museum

**Sandcastles**

**Sandcastles**

**Street cleaner in boat**

# The Doughnut

# END OF THE PIER SHOW

**Winter sun**

**Fire**

**Calm**

**Shipwreck**

# **BRIGHTON TOWN**

**Old Steine bikers**

## Old Crocks' race

# Climbing home

# Haircut

## Pavilion Gardens

**Pavilion Gardens**

**North Laines buskers**

**Springtime**

# Football

**Engineerium**

**Doggy Fashion**

**Doggy fashion**

**Duke of York cinema**

**Café Motu**

**Museum**

**Library reflections**

# **FESTIVAL FROLICS**

**Spiegel Tent**

**Spiegel Tent**

**Crowds on Colonnade**

**Disc Jockey**

**Fiddler, Chapel Royal**

**Wild Park Fiesta**

**Dog meets seagull**

**Glider**

# **BEYOND BRIGHTON**

**Lewes**

# Kingston

# Adur Valley

**Cuckmere Haven**

# The Downs

# The Chattri

**Rottingdean Beach**

**Pond above Falmer**

## On Worthing Pier

**Worthing Pier**

## Shoreham Boathouse

# Shoreham Airport

**Shoreham Harbour**

## Shoreham Harbour

## Shoreham hull

**De la Warr Pavilion**

# The Camel at Glynde

# The Cuckoo Trail

**Rouen Museum**

**Dieppe Harbour**

# Cooking under the Arches

# Cooking under the Arches

The Normans arrived in Sussex with a sophisticated cuisine. Noodles flavoured with sugar and ginger, coloured with saffron and grated with cheese. 'Jelly', a dish of poached pig, spiced with galangale and set in white wine. 'Gravey', a sauce of almonds and ginger, popular with rabbit, oysters and eel. 'Pottage', the vegetable patch that produced a wholesome soup, and 'rose pottage', a delicate infusion of petals in almond milk. Pastries made from chestnut flour and filled with honeyed pine nuts. Dishes of invention that would grace a modern table.

Much of Sussex food has its roots in the sea. In 1653, Izzak Walton identified the four 'good things' of Sussex as 'a Shelsey cockle, a Chichester lobster, an Arundel mullet and an Amberley trout'. Oysters were cheap and plentiful until disease wiped them out. Scallops, equally abundant, have almost died away, but you can still come across a local variety known as 'Queenies'. As the link with the land was lost and agriculture industrialised, many indigenous foods disappeared. Samphire, or sea spinach, once colonised the cliff tops, leaves eaten raw for salad, stalks cooked like asparagus. West Sussex was famous for hunting truffles, and the whole county was renowned for its diversity of apples. The name 'Golden Pippin' came from a gift of Sussex apples sent to Catherine the Great, each fruit wrapped in golden paper. Other evocative varieties – 'The Sussex Five Bells', 'The Gooseberry Knock-Out', 'The Sussex Greenlanes' – are all extinct, along with the centuries old tradition of making cider.

The turn of the Millennium has seen something of a renaissance of local food. 'The Sussex Food Finder' contains an impressive list of farms that produce real meat, organic cheese, homemade preserves and pies. Sussex was once synonymous with pies and puddings, just about every food finding its way inside a suet crust. The most parsimonious pudding was a salted mixture of flour and water known as 'Hard Dick'. We never knowingly offered 'Hard Dick' to the public at 'The Cook and Fiddle', but did attempt to present a taste of Sussex.

# *Starters*

## *Fish soup*

A very tenuous thread maintains the tradition of Brighton fishing, with only a dozen boats still fishing out of the Marina. On the seafront I was lucky to work close to Carol and Alan's fish shop, selling the local catch of the day. At first the variety came as a surprise, red mullet and sea bream plentiful in the summer, and squid for a sauce calamari. For years I experimented with Mediterranean fish for a bouillabaisse, but the expensive ingredients never seemed to produce much in the way of taste. Then I stumbled on the idea of using Huss, and at last success was at hand. Huss looks an unpromising choice, long eel-like body and a ferociously rough skin, but the secret lies in teasing a gelatinous stock from the bone. Carol's stall has now passed on to her nephew Neil.

Ingredients: 6-8 portions
1 kilo of Huss
250 gm onions
6 cloves of garlic
300 ml of wine, half red, half white.
250 gm tinned tomatoes
Juice of a lemon
Salt, pepper and Tabasco

Method:
1/ Cut the Huss into 6" lengths and remove the flesh from the central bone.

Place the bone in a pan with a couple of cods' heads, cover with water and simmer gently for 40 minutes. Strain the stock and set aside.

2/ Peel and roughly chop the onions and garlic, and sweat down in a little oil. Add the fish, seasoning, lemon juice and wine. Increase the heat for a few minutes to reduce the wine then add the tomatoes and enough stock to produce a thick soup.

Simmer gently under cover for 40 minutes.

3/ Pass the soup through a blender. Serve with toasted slices of baguette and grated gruyère cheese.

~ ~ ~ ~ ~ ~ ~ ~ ~ ~ ~ ~ ~ ~ ~

## *Carrot and butterbean soup*

A firm favourite on wild, windswept days. You could look out from the arch at the waves pounding the shingle, sheltered in the eye of the storm.

> Ingredients: 6-8 portions
> 500 gm dried butterbeans, soaked overnight
> 500 gm carrots
> 250 gm onions
> Half a head of garlic
> 100 ml vegetable oil
> 2 pints semi-skimmed milk (approximately)
> Teaspoon marmite
> Salt, pepper, nutmeg

Method:

1/ Drain and rinse the butterbeans. Place in a pan, cover with water and simmer for 40 minutes or until almost tender. Stir in a teaspoon of marmite during cooking.

2/ Peel and roughly chop the onions, garlic and carrots. Sweat down in oil and add the cooked butterbeans along with their cooking liquid. Pour in enough milk to make a thick soup, add seasoning and simmer gently under a loose lid for 40 minutes.

3/ Pass through a liquidiser, re-heat and serve.

~ ~ ~ ~ ~ ~ ~ ~ ~ ~ ~ ~ ~ ~ ~

## Chicken liver pâté with apple & cinnamon

I got this idea during a 'stage' at Michel Guérards' restaurant in the Landes district of France, where chicken livers were garnished with sautéed slices of apple. The garnish was a fragile affair, and it occurred to me that it would be much simpler to combine the ingredients in a pâté.

Ingredients:
500 gm of chicken livers
150 gm of onion
150 gm of cooking apple
100ml of apple juice and/or brandy
50 ml sunflower oil
Cinnamon, salt & pepper.

Method:
1/ Remove the gristly bits from the livers.
2/ Finely dice the onion and sweat down in a little oil. Throw in the chicken livers and sauté and fry on all sides.
3/ Peel, quarter and core the apple. Add to the pan with seasoning and cinnamon. When the apple has softened, pour in the apple juice or brandy. Cook out for a few minutes.
4/ Pass swiftly through a blender, retaining a grainy texture. Chill.
5/ Serve with buttered toast

~ ~ ~ ~ ~ ~ ~ ~ ~ ~ ~ ~ ~ ~ ~

## *Homemade hummus*

Real hummus is simple to make, and bears little resemblance to the watery supermarket product. It was the main ingredient of our 'Mediterranean sunshine salad'; including olive bread, tabbouleh, and all the fruit and leaves the summer had to offer.

Ingredients:
500 gm of dried chickpeas, left to soak overnight in cold water
70 gm or two dessert spoons of dark tahini (sesame seed paste)
Lemon juice to taste
1 teaspoon salt
150 ml sunflower oil
150 ml olive oil
4 cloves of garlic

Method:
1/ Drain and rinse the chickpeas. Bring to the boil and skim off the scum. Cook until tender. Drain and rinse again,
2/ Add all the ingredients to a blender. If it is a small machine, you may need to make two batches. This is quite a thick mixture, so you will need to scrape down the bowl every 30 seconds. The amount of oil is only a guide; if the mixture is too dry add some more.
3/ Chill in a covered container.

~ ~ ~ ~ ~ ~ ~ ~ ~ ~ ~ ~ ~ ~ ~

## *Taramasalata*

This is also simple to make, but unlike shop-bought varieties, actually tastes of smoked fish! The addition of cream cheese is an idea from George Lassalle, 'The Adventurous Fish Cook'. Tarama goes well on a warm, chewy bagel from Julian the Brighton 'Bagelman'.

'Springs' of Henfield have been smoking all things fish for the past 30 years. Further up the price ladder, 'The Weald Smokery' at Flimwell smokes game and sausages as well as fish. They produce seriously luxurious hampers at Xmas time.

Ingredients:
500 gm smoked cods roe
Juice of 1 lemon
200 ml sunflower oil (approximately)
150 gm cream cheese

Method:
1/ Remove all the roe from the skin and put into a blender along with the lemon juice, cream cheese and half the oil.

2/ Whirl the mixture, scraping down every 30 seconds. Gradually add more oil until you're happy with the consistency. Don't add salt as the smoked roes are often over salted.

3/ Chill and serve on toast or a bagel.

~ ~ ~ ~ ~ ~ ~ ~ ~ ~ ~ ~ ~ ~ ~

## *Sussex cheeses with walnut and raisin bread*

We used to offer 'Sussex cheese platter' as a starter, with a few choice radishes and a good wholesome bread. There is a primeval quality to the process of making bread, and this one is sweet and nutty. For local cheese suppliers look up the 'Good Food Directory' at the end of this chapter.

Ingredients: Makes 1 loaf.
200 gm wholemeal flour
150 gm strong white flour
80 gm walnuts
80 gm raisins
300 ml warm water
15 gm fresh yeast
30 ml vegetable oil
Teaspoon of honey
1 egg
Good pinch of salt.

Method:
1/ Set the oven to 200°c, gas mark 6. Brush a loaf tin with oil, line with greaseproof paper and brush again.
2/ Chop the walnuts into little chunks. Place in a large bowl with the flour, salt and raisins and leave in a warm place.
3/ Stir the honey into the warm water and pour a little over the yeast. Leave to stand for a few minutes, then stir to a smooth paste. Combine with the dry ingredients and add

sufficient water until the dough is moist but not sticky. Knead vigorously for 5 minutes; cover the bowl with a wet cloth and leave to stand in a warm place for 90 minutes.

4/ Give the dough a hearty thump, a process known as 'knocking back', and knead well for 5 minutes, pulling and stretching the elastic paste. Place the dough in the loaf tin so it is about two thirds full. Cover loosely with a wet tea towel and leave to prove for another hour.

5/ Brush with egg wash and bake for half an hour. Remove from the tin and bake a further 10 minutes at 180°c. Allow to stand on a cooling wire. Best enjoyed when still slightly warm and moist.

~ ~ ~ ~ ~ ~ ~ ~ ~ ~ ~ ~ ~ ~

# *Fish*

## *Local chargrilled fish*

If you can get hold of really fresh fish, the simpler the cooking, the better. The fish will always taste sweet, the chargrill imparting a scorched, smoky flavour. Brush the fish with oil and make sure the grill or barbecue is very hot. Flat fish takes about three minutes on each side, round fish a little longer.

It just remains to decide on an accompanying sauce. Sauce Provencal suits almost every fish. Sweat down lots of onion and garlic in a little oil, toss in a tin of chopped tomatoes, a dash of Tabasco and some dry white wine. Season and simmer under cover for half an hour. Liquidise in the blender, re-heat and serve with a twist of lemon. When used to gently braise squid or cuttlefish, sauce Provencal produces a tender dish unlike the rubber rings of deep-fried calamari.

<u>Watercress sauce</u> goes well with delicate flavoured fish, such as lemon sole. Chop off the thick stalks from a bunch of watercress, and blanch in boiling water for 30 seconds. Drain, roughly chop and set aside. Dice two onions and sweat down in oil under cover on a gentle heat. When softened, stir in a tablespoon of flour and a spoon of grainy mustard. Gradually incorporate half a pint of milk, or a mixture of milk and fish stock. Add the watercress. Season with salt, pepper and nutmeg, bring to a simmer and cook gently for 15 minutes. Pass through the blender, reheat and serve.

<u>Oily fish</u> such as herring or mackerel, go well with <u>gooseberry or rhubarb sauce.</u> The tartness of the fruit cuts through the astringent flavour of the fish. Top and tail the gooseberries, and simmer gently in a little water till almost puréed. There is no need to season or pass through a blender. With rhubarb, simply chop and cook till soft in a little water. Rhubarb is also a surprisingly good accompaniment with salmon.

<u>Tuna</u> has a really full flavour, almost like gamey meat. Fresh tuna is very expensive, but you can get perfectly good frozen tuna steaks that are much cheaper. They grill extremely well and look impressive with a criss-cross effect from the bars of the chargrill. Quite by accident, I discovered that coq au vin sauce is a brilliant match for tuna. At the end of work one day, I cooked some tuna for the staff and served it up with leftover coq au vin. The smoky bacon and red wine

sauce complements the strong flavour of tuna. The recipe follows on page 153.

~ ~ ~ ~ ~ ~ ~ ~ ~ ~ ~ ~ ~ ~ ~

# *Mackerel marinated in white wine*

The Omega 3 fatty acid content of mackerel makes it a health food 'par excellence'. What is more, it is ridiculously cheap. If you don't want to smoke the place out grilling mackerel, try marinating it. It keeps for ages, and you can even use the old marinade to top up a new batch. Logically, the flavour can only intensify with each renewed use, but after a month or so, I make a concession to modern hygiene management, and toss the marinade away.

> Ingredients: 6 portions
> 6 mackerel, filleted.
> Juice of 1 lemon
> 300 ml water
> 300 ml dry white wine
> 300 ml wine vinegar
> 3 onions
> 3 carrots
> Bay leaves, peppercorns, salt

Method:

1/ Brush a large oven proof container with oil. Lay the fillets, skin side down, and set aside.

2/ Chop the onions into rings and the carrots into batons. Place in a saucepan with all the seasoning and pour in all the recipe liquid. You may want to alter the proportions of wine and wine vinegar, depending on how tart you want the marinade. Personally I prefer a delicate flavour that is not too acidic. Bring the mixture to the boil and simmer gently for half an hour.

3/ Pour the marinade over the fillets, and leave immersed for 5-10 minutes. Using a fish slice, carefully lift the fillets into the container you are going to store them in. When the marinade is luke-warm, pour over the fillets. When cool, cover and refrigerate.

4/ Serve with chunky brown bread or potato salad. Decorate with the onion rings, carrots and bay leaf.

~ ~ ~ ~ ~ ~ ~ ~ ~ ~ ~ ~ ~ ~ ~

## *Plaice with banana and ginger.*

This is a dish that featured on Festival nights, when a special dinner was accompanied with live music. We had quite a variety of acts over the years; blues guitar, lively cello, a butterfly flight of violin and flute. My favourite was a young harpist who filled the arch with golden sound, the gentle plucking soothing away every trace of jagged thoughts.

Ingredients: 4 portions
2 large plaice, filleted
100 ml vegetable oil
Juice of 1 lemon
2 bananas
1 piece of ginger

Method:
1 /Set the oven to gas mark 6, 200°c. Brush an ovenproof dish with oil.

2/ Peel the ginger and chop very finely. Soften in a little oil. Mix with the lemon juice, sliced bananas and a little salt. Fold this mixture inside the fillets and lay in the earthenware. Cover with foil and bake for 20 minutes.

3/ Accompany with saffron rice and a green salad. For real luxury, serve with a scallop, shallow-fried on both sides.

~ ~ ~ ~ ~ ~ ~ ~ ~ ~ ~ ~ ~ ~ ~

## *Cod with cashews, coriander and coconut*

I got the idea for this recipe from Jane Grigson, one in a great line of English women cookery writers that began with Elizabeth David. Eons ago, when I taught food studies at Bournemouth University, Jane Grigson came to deliver a lecture to the students. She extolled the virtues of simple food, such as local cheese with homemade bread, and condemned developments that have adulterated the food chain. This recipe is full of authentic flavours.

Ingredients: Serves 8
1 kilo of cod fillet
8 king prawns
100 ml vegetable oil
250 gm onions
4 cloves of garlic
450 gm tomato
100 gm cashews
Coconut milk (Oriental food shops sell it in a block)
50 gm desiccated coconut
1 bunch of fresh coriander. Salt & pepper.

Method:
1/ Set the oven to 190º, mark 5. Toast the cashews till lightly brown.

2/ Shell the prawns and make a stock with the shells and the cods' head.

3/ Peel and chop the onions and garlic. Peel the tomatoes

by making a small incision at the mark of the stalk. Plunge into boiling water for 20 seconds, remove and the skins should peel away easily. Roughly chop the pulp.

4/ Soak the coriander to remove any grit and leave to drain. Remove the thick stalks and roughly chop the leaves.

5/ Soften the onion and garlic in a little oil. Add the tomatoes and enough stock and coconut milk to make a sauce consistency. Add the desiccated coconut and most of the coriander and simmer for 20 minutes.

Brush an ovenproof dish with oil and lay the cod fillets inside. Sprinkle with cashew nuts, salt and pepper. Pour over the sauce, cover with foil and bake for 25 minutes.

5/ Garnish with the king prawns and the remaining coriander. Serve with rice cooked in coconut milk.

~ ~ ~ ~ ~ ~ ~ ~ ~ ~ ~ ~ ~ ~

# *Birds & game*

## *Coq au vin*

It's hard to find a real cock these days. Instead, buy a chicken from a butcher like 'Archers' in Hanover, a bird that has strutted about the farmyard a bit, preening and pecking like a Kemptown queen. The last time I was in the shop Mr Archer informed me of an old Sussex lamb dish called 'Lookers Pie'. Shepherds used to employ 'lookers' to help watch the flock; two good lookers and your life was complete.

Ingredients: 4 portions
1 free-range/organic/corn-fed chicken or even guinea fowl.

100 gm smoked back bacon
100 ml sunflower oil
40 gm flour
4 cloves of garlic
150 gm onion
150 gm button mushrooms
300 ml red wine
300 ml chicken stock

Method:

1/ Dissect the legs and breasts from the carcass. Cover and set aside in the bottom of the fridge. Place the carcass and giblets in a large saucepan, along with some root vegetables and peppercorns. Cover with water and simmer very gently for four hours, skimming off the grease and scum. Strain the stock.

2/ Finely dice the onions and garlic and sweat down in a little oil along with thinly cut strips of bacon. Stir in the flour and gradually incorporate the stock and wine. Add the chicken pieces, season and either cook slowly under cover on the stove, or in a casserole in a moderate oven. After half an hour add the mushrooms. Cooking should take about one and a half hours, depending on the size of the chicken.

3/ A good accompaniment is 'pomme boulangère'. Thinly slice potatoes and onions and braise in the oven, half covered with milk and chicken stock. This takes about as long to cook as the chicken.

~ ~ ~ ~ ~ ~ ~ ~ ~ ~ ~ ~ ~ ~

## *Herby lemon chicken*

This is a much lighter chicken dish with a fromage blanc stuffing that infuses its flavour under the skin. Fromage frais can also be used, but in the absence of both, try a combination of smooth yoghurt and cottage cheese. Many recipes combine tarragon with chicken, but my favourite herb is marjoram. Once established in the garden, it should come back every year.

>Ingredients: 4 portions
>I free range chicken
>300 ml fromage blanc
>Juice of 1 lemon
>Fresh marjoram and flat leaf parsley
>100 gm mushrooms
>Salt, pepper, nutmeg.

Method:
1/ Set the oven to 200c, mark 6. With your index finger, carefully ease away the skin from the chicken breasts, taking care not to tear the skin. Place the chicken in a lightly oiled roasting tray.

2/ Chop the parsley and mushrooms very finely. Combine in a bowl with all the other ingredients. Using a teaspoon, carefully insert some of this mixture inside the pouch you have made above each breast. Cover the roasting tray with foil and cook for approximately 80 minutes, occasionally basting the skin.

3/ Set aside the chicken and pour all the cooking juices

into a bowl. Allow to stand for a while and spoon off the fat that settles on the surface. Return the juices and remaining fromage blanc mixture to the roasting tray. Place on the stove, stirring vigorously with a wooden spoon to incorporate all the caramelised sediment. This forms the sauce to accompany the chicken.

Add any chicken juice that accumulates while the bird is resting.

4/ Quarter the chicken and serve with honeyed carrots and broccoli florets.

~ ~ ~ ~ ~ ~ ~ ~ ~ ~ ~ ~ ~ ~

## *Rabbit with plums*

Rabbits abound on the Downs, and Archers supply local rabbit and venison at different times of the year. The plums complement the flavour of rabbit which is sweet rather than gamey.

Ingredients: 4 portions
1 rabbit – get your butcher to joint it.
300 gm purple plums
200 gm onions
175 ml dry white wine
75 ml port
Sprig of rosemary
200 ml rabbit stock

Method:

1/ Put the head and giblets into a saucepan. Cover with water, bring to the boil and simmer gently for an hour. Strain the stock and set aside.

2/ Sweat down the onions in a little oil. Add the rabbit pieces, increase the heat and pour in the alcohol.

3/ Stone the plums, add to the pan with the rosemary, pour in the stock and season. Simmer gently under cover, for about 45 minutes.

4/ Remove the rabbit and set aside. Purée the sauce in a blender, and return to the pan to reheat the rabbit. Serve with mashed potato.

~ ~ ~ ~ ~ ~ ~ ~ ~ ~ ~ ~ ~ ~ ~

## *Venison stew*

This sauce includes the South American touch of adding a small amount of bitter chocolate. I gleaned this tip from the surreal novel by Laura Esquivel, 'Like water for chocolate', where the heroine farts herself to death on the toilet.
A demise not to be replicated in a restaurant.

> Ingredients: 4 portions
> 700 gm stewing venison
> 100 ml vegetable oil
> 200 gm onions
> 200 gm carrots
> 3 cloves garlic
> 40 gm flour
> 200 ml red wine
> 200 ml meat stock
> 2 cubes of very bitter chocolate

Method:

1/ Cube the meat, removing any fatty bits. Venison is in fact a very lean source of red meat.

2/ Finely chop the onions and garlic. Soften in a little oil and add the venison. Lightly brown and then dust with flour, stirring over a gentle heat for 2 minutes. Gradually incorporate the wine and stock and some salt & pepper. Finally toss in the sliced carrots.

3/ Allow to simmer very gently, under cover for an hour. Adjust seasoning to taste, and just before service stir in the chocolate. Serve with sweet potato purée. – see vegetarian recipes, page 165.

~ ~ ~ ~ ~ ~ ~ ~ ~ ~ ~ ~ ~ ~ ~

## *Duck with lemon and lavender honey*

Recipes involving meat or poultry stock are difficult for the home cook as the stock requires hours of cooking, and the dank smell permeates every corner of the house. The stock in this recipe can be made in an hour. The fat that drains from the duck makes the best roast potatoes in the world.

Ingredients: 4 portions
1 large duck with giblets
1 large onion
200 ml white wine
100 ml lavender honey
Juice of 2 lemons

Method:
1/ Set the oven on high. Cut off the winglets and place in a pan with the giblets and diced onion. Cover with water and wine, bring to a simmer and skim off the froth. Simmer gently for an hour.

2/ Place the duck in a roasting tray and put in the hot oven. After 20 minutes reduce the heat to mark 5 or 190ºc. Every 20-30 minutes, prick the skin all over, taking care not to pierce the flesh. Pour off the fat which can be used for roasting potatoes. Any juices that settle under the fat should be added to the sauce. The bird should be cooked in about an hour and a quarter, or when the juices run dark from the cavity. My Czech grandma had a majestic way with duck and goose. To get especially crisp skin, she spooned a little cold water over the bird for the final 10 minutes in the oven.

3/ Strain the stock and reduce the liquid over a high heat. Squeeze the lemons and add half the juice, a good spoon of honey and some seasoning. When the liquid has reduced by half, taste and reduce further if the flavour is insipid. Add more lemon or honey according to what is needed. The sauce is ready when it tastes ducky, tangy and slightly sweet.

4/ A large duck just about serves 4 people. Dissect the legs, remove the breasts and slice thinly. This way each guest gets some magret and some leg meat. Serve with the sauce.

5/ As well as roast potatoes, an ideal accompaniment is <u>fruity red cabbage.</u> Cut a cabbage in half and remove the woody core and any wilted outer leaves. Chop the cabbage finely and place in a pan with a large diced onion, a large diced cooking apple, a handful of raisins, salt and pepper. Moisten with apple juice and a little wine vinegar. Stir in a good spoonful of honey. Simmer gently on a very low heat until the cabbage has softened.

~ ~ ~ ~ ~ ~ ~ ~ ~ ~ ~ ~ ~ ~

# vegetarian dishes

## Vegetable stir fry with lemon grass and halloumi

Our Norman ancestors discovered spices when they marauded down to Arabia. Today it is simpler visiting 'Yum Yum' in Sydney Street. For stir fries I like to use a combination of ginger, garlic and lemon grass, and if liquid is required, a good vegetable stock rather than soya sauce. The Sussex High Weald dairy farm near Duddleswell makes excellent organic sheep cheeses. Halloumi has a texture similar to mozzarella, and if added to the wok at the end of a stir fry, soaks up the tasty juices. We once visited the farm for an end of season outing. 'Sussex Slipcote' is a creamy log flavoured with garlic or peppercorns. There is also organic Duddleswell, feta and smoked 'Ashdown Forester'. We finished off proceedings with a trip to the village tea shop, and a delicious selection of pies.

Ingredients:

Whatever vegetables are in season, offering a combination of flavour, colour and texture.

Vegetable stock

Olive oil

Handful of ginger, head of garlic, 6 sticks of lemon grass.

Chinese noodles or long grain rice.

Method:

1/ Simmer some root vegetables in water for an hour. Strain and reserve the stock

2/ Peel the garlic and ginger, and remove the woody tops from the lemon grass. Finely chop all the ingredients, and fry in a wok in hot olive oil. After two minutes, add a few ladlefuls of stock, and continue cooking till most of the liquid has evaporated. Turn into a blender, and whir until you achieve a smooth paste. Covered in oil, this mixture will keep in the fridge for a week.

3/ To make the stir fry, cut your vegetables into bite-size chunks. Heat some oil in the wok and add one spoonful of the spicy mix per person. Gradually add the vegetables, thickest ones first, shaking the pan regularly. Serve on a bed of noodles or cooked rice. Briefly toss the sliced halloumi in the wok to soak up the spicy flavour. Arrange the cheese on top of the vegetables and garnish with a twist of orange.

~ ~ ~ ~ ~ ~ ~ ~ ~ ~ ~ ~ ~ ~ ~

## *Coriander chickpea ragoût with sweet potato purée.*

Like most stews, the flavour improves with a few days storage in the fridge. This dish provides variations on the palette orange to red, with tomato, chickpea and sweet potato. Orange denotes carotene in fruit and vegetables, so this dish is rich in Vitamin A.

Ingredients: 4-6 portions
250 gm onions
5 cloves garlic
100 ml olive oil
Seasoning, tabasco
450 gm tin of tomatoes
250 gm dried chickpeas, soaked overnight
200 gm mushrooms
200 gm courgettes
Bunch of fresh coriander
200 ml smooth yoghurt or double cream

For the purée:
1 kilo sweet potatoes
30 gm butter
50 ml semi-skimmed milk
Salt and black pepper

Method:
1/ Dice the onions and garlic, and soften in olive oil on a gentle heat! Add the tomatoes, seasoning & tabasco. Simmer

gently for half an hour and pass through the blender.

2/ Drain and rinse the chickpeas. Boil till tender then drain and rinse again.

3/ Wash and slice the courgettes and mushrooms. Soak the coriander to remove any grit, drain, remove the thick stalks and chop finely.

4/ Pour the tomato sauce and all the above ingredients into a pan. Simmer under cover for 40 minutes, adjust seasoning and stir in the yoghurt or cream. If using yoghurt stir in off the heat or it may separate.

5/ Scrub the sweet potatoes, cut into suitable size and immerse in boiling water. Drain when tender and remove the skin. Mash with butter and a little milk. Serve with the chickpea ragoût.

~ ~ ~ ~ ~ ~ ~ ~ ~ ~ ~ ~ ~ ~ ~

## *Roast parsnip and carrot strudel with a wild mushroom sauce*

This is a good dish to make in the autumn when all the vegetable ingredients are in season. You rarely see fresh strudel pastry made these days, but it is very light, fun to make, and you can use it to wrap up any combination of sweet or savoury foods. Long before sugar became affordable, the Norman invaders valued parsnips for their sweetness; the pulp squeezed and added to dishes much like honey.

Ingredients: 6 portions
Strudel paste: 230 gm strong white flour
1 whole egg. 1 egg yolk.
100 ml milk
50 gm melted butter

Filling:
500gm carrots
30 ml honey
50 gm butter
500 gm parsnips
250 gm onions
100 ml vegetable oil

Method:
1/ Set the oven to 180°c, mark 5. Place the flour and eggs in a bowl. Gradually incorporate the milk and half the melted butter. Turn out onto a surface and knead until you obtain a

smooth, elastic dough. Lightly dust with flour, cover with a bowl and leave to rest for an hour.

2/ Peel and halve the parsnips and onions. Place in a roasting tray and baste with hot oil. Roast till tender.

3/ Peel and slice the carrots. Place in a pan with honey, butter, salt & pepper and half cover with water. Cook on a hot stove and when the water has evaporated, turn out into a bowl. Roughly chop along with the roasted onion and parsnip and return to the bowl.

4/ Roll the strudel paste into a rectangle; you will need to be patient as the elasticity of the strong flour will cause the dough to shrink after each rolling. When the paste is as thin as possible, get someone to help you. Standing on opposite sides of a table, place your hands under the dough until your fingertips touch. Draw your hands towards you so that the dough is gently stretched. Carry on until you can see your fingers through the dough.

Lift the dough onto a tea towel dusted with flour. Square off any mis-shapen edges with a big kitchen knife.

5/ Spread the vegetables over the dough, leaving an inch border all around. Brush the four borders with butter, and fold over the filling. Holding the ends of the tea towel tightly, roll the strudel up like a swiss roll. Lift onto a baking tray and brush with butter. Bake for 30-40 minutes.

6/ Serve with the following wild mushroom sauce.

~ ~ ~ ~ ~ ~ ~ ~ ~ ~ ~ ~ ~ ~ ~

## *Wild mushroom sauce*

This is an indispensable component of vegetarian cookery, providing moisture for the ubiquitous nut roast and a tasty pasta sauce. When I lived in Rouen, mountains of mushrooms would appear at market in the autumn, little orange girolles on gangly stalks and dense, fleshy ceps. Dried mushrooms are a perfectly good product, just make sure you soak and rinse them well to get rid of any grit.

Ingredients:
100 ml olive oil
200 gm onions
30 gm flour
4 cloves of garlic
150 gm wild mushrooms
250 gm field mushrooms
Salt, pepper, nutmeg
300 ml milk
300 ml vegetable stock
50 ml Madeira

Method:
1/ Wash, drain and slice the mushrooms.
2/ Finely chop the onions and garlic, and soften under cover in the olive oil. Stir in the flour and cook gently for a couple of minutes. Gradually incorporate the recipe liquid then stir in the mushrooms and seasoning. Simmer gently for 20 minutes.

3/ Serve chunky or blend in a blender

~ ~ ~ ~ ~ ~ ~ ~ ~ ~ ~ ~ ~ ~ ~

## *Veggie crêpes*

This was an all time favourite on the seafront. All three components can be made in advance, the filling, the cheese sauce and the pancakes. The idea is to get a light crêpe, and using a proportion of Doves Farm wholemeal flour, you can achieve this with the bonus of added texture. Buy the flour at Infinity foods. It is essential to get the crêpe pan really hot and then swill the batter round so it is just coating the surface of the pan. It is a skill that comes with practice, and soon you will be comfortable working two pans at once. If you can get hold of a black iron pan all the better; they never need washing and last for ever.

A leek & mushroom filling is described here, but the sauce should change with the season. When courgettes and aubergines are plentiful in the summer, a ratatouille filling goes well with the cheese topping.

Ingredients for the crêpe batter: 8 portions
120 gm Doves Farm light wholemeal flour
120 gm white flour
2 eggs
600 ml semi-skimmed milk
100 ml sunflower oil

Method:
1/ Beat the eggs into the flour, and gradually incorporate the milk. To avoid a lumpy batter, beat hard until all the flour is combined into a smooth paste. Thereafter it is an easier job to combine the remaining milk. Rest in the fridge for an hour.

2/ Place a brush in a little jug of oil. Anoint the pan with oil, and when almost smoking, swirl a small ladleful of batter around the pan. Return the pan to the heat and after 30 seconds, bang the pan on the stove. Edge around the sides with a palette knife, and flip the pancake over.

3/ When both sides are done, turn out onto a plate. You can pile successive pancakes on top of each other.

~ ~ ~ ~ ~ ~ ~ ~ ~ ~ ~ ~ ~ ~ ~

## *Leek and mushroom sauce*

Ingredients: 1 kilo of leeks
250 gm mushrooms
250 gm onions
100 ml sunflower oil
60 gm wholemeal flour
1 pint semi-skimmed milk
Salt, pepper, nutmeg

Method:
1/ Discard the roots and the tough green ends of the leeks. Cut the leeks in half lengthways, and slice finely. Immerse in a plentiful amount of cold water, lift out and drain. With muddy leeks this process may have to be repeated

2/ Wash, drain and slice the mushrooms

3/ Chop the onions and sweat down with the leeks in some oil. When softened, remove the lid and stir in the flour. Gradually incorporate the milk, adding more as the sauce thickens. Add the mushrooms and seasoning and simmer gently for 20 minutes, stirring regularly.

~~~~~~~~~~~~~~~~

## *Mornay sauce for the topping*

>70gm butter or 70 ml oil
>70gm flour
>Spoonful of grainy mustard
>1 litre semi-skimmed milk
>Salt and pepper
>200 gm mature cheddar cheese, grated.

Method:

1/ Heat the oil or butter in a pan and stir in the flour and mustard. Cook gently for 2 minutes and gradually incorporate the milk. Bring to a simmer and cook gently, stirring occasionally, for 10 minutes. Add seasoning.

2/ Take off the heat and stir in the grated cheese.

~~~~~~~~~~~~~~~~

## *Compiling the Veggie Crêpe*

It is easier if the filling has been made in advance and chilled. Spoon some filling into a crêpe, and roll into a fat cigar shape. Place the filled pancakes in an earthenware dish and coat with the warm cheese sauce. Heat through in a medium oven or a microwave. Serve with a crisp salad dressed with vinaigrette. For a good flavour combine 2 parts walnut oil with 1 part raspberry vinegar, and a little grainy mustard.

~ ~ ~ ~ ~ ~ ~ ~ ~ ~ ~ ~ ~ ~ ~

# *Afternoon tea*

## *Apricot scones*

Weeks could pass at the 'Cook & Fiddle' without selling a solitary scone. Then the beach would go teapot crazy, people mesmerised by the paraphernalia of laden trays. The staff hated cream teas; tiny tips, mountains of dishes and the urn on the verge of a breakdown. Vera never recovered from her first shift, when an influx of 30 Chinese students arrived unannounced, for the full Sussex Monty. She unsuspectingly served a plateful of scones I'd just dug out of the freezer. The platter retrieved in a Fawltyesque swoop, re-appearing oven fresh from the microwave.

Ingredients: – makes about a dozen
450 gm self raising flour
1 teaspoon of baking powder
60 gm of dry apricots (partially re-hydrated are best)
100 gm butter
60 gm caster sugar
200 ml semi-skimmed milk
1 egg

Method:
1/ Set the oven to 190c, Mark 5.

2/ Cube the butter and cream together with the sugar and finely chopped apricots. Add the flour and baking powder, and rub together until you get bread crumb consistency.

3/ Gradually incorporate the milk to make a cohesive dough. Roll out to about 5cm in depth, brush with egg wash and cut out with a 6cm pastry cutter. Roll up the remaining dough and repeat the process. Space out the scones on a baking tray and bake for about 12-15 minutes, or when the bottom of the scone produces a hollow sound when tapped.

4/ Place on a cooling wire. Serve with clotted cream and jam, or the following variation made with fresh fruit. Cook a punnet of strawberries or raspberries in a little fruit juice and a dollop of honey. When the fruit is softened, turn out to cool. Meanwhile, whip some double cream and fold in the fruit and juice. Slice the scones and spread generously.

~ ~ ~ ~ ~ ~ ~ ~ ~ ~ ~ ~ ~ ~ ~

## *Fruity fruitcake*

This is the ultimate healthy cake. There is no added sugar, all the sweetness comes from dried fruit which also supplies plentiful amounts of fibre.

Ingredients: – Makes two cakes
220 gm pitted dates
1 kilo of mixed dried fruit – raisins, sultanas etc.
350 gm wholemeal flour
3 teaspoons of baking powder
4 eggs
1 teaspoon ground nutmeg and 2 teaspoons of cinnamon

Method:
1/ Brush two loaf tins with oil. Line with greaseproof and brush again. Set the oven to 160c, gas mark 4.

2/ Roughly chop the dates, just to make sure there are no stray stones. Place in a saucepan, half cover with water, and bring to a gentle simmer. When most of the liquid has been absorbed, pass through a blender, and leave to cool.

2/ Separate the eggs and add the yolks to the dates. Blend to a purée.

3/ Place the mixed dried fruit in a bowl, and sieve the flour, cinnamon, nutmeg and baking powder over the fruit. Finally return the bran to the bowl. Stir the ingredients so that all the fruit is coated with flour, then combine with the date mixture.

4/ Whisk the egg whites to soft peaks. Pour the cake mixture on top of the whites, and combine well with a large kitchen spoon. Pour into loaf tins, and place in the oven. After half an hour, loosely cover with foil. The cakes are done when a sharp knife comes clean from the centre. Cooking time should be between 60-90 minutes. Turn out onto a cooling wire and peel away the greaseproof.

~ ~ ~ ~ ~ ~ ~ ~ ~ ~ ~ ~ ~ ~ ~

## *Baked hazelnut cheesecake*

The average gelatinous cheesecake is a foam of creamy sugar. This cake is lower in fat and the baking infuses the base with the aroma of toasted hazelnuts.

Ingredients: 1 cake
8 plain digestive biscuits
60 gm hazelnuts
50 gm melted butter
2 eggs
500 gm fromage blanc or fromage frais
30 gm flour
30 gm caster sugar
50 gm dried fruit, apricots or raisins roughly chopped

Method:
1/ Set the oven to 190c, Mark 5. Take a 28 cm cake ring with releasable bottom, and brush with oil.

2/ Toast the hazelnuts, and when cool, rub together to remove the skins. Place in a blender with the biscuits, and whir so the nuts are still a bit chunky. Turn into a bowl, and combine with the melted butter. Spoon into the cake ring, pressing down well.

3/ Separate the eggs and stir the yolks in with the fromage blanc, flour, sugar and dried fruit. Beat well.

4/ Whisk the egg whites to soft peaks. Pour the fromage blanc mixture onto the whites, and combine well. Pour over the biscuit base and place in the oven. The cake will be baked in about 45 minutes. Allow to cool, cut round the edge and remove the outer ring. Do not worry if the surface cracks a bit during cooling, as you can camouflage this with a fresh fruit garnish. Sliced kiwi and black grapes in winter; strawberries in summer.

~ ~ ~ ~ ~ ~ ~ ~ ~ ~ ~ ~ ~ ~ ~

## *Little apple choux buns*

Choux is miraculous. Who would believe that a pastry beginning with fat melted in water, then thickened to a stodgy paste, would eventually emerge from the oven a crisp light shell.

Ingredients: 10 portions
For the pastry-
100 gm butter
125 gm strong flour
3 eggs
Half a pint of water

For the filling-
500 gm thick smooth yoghurt
750 gm cooking apples
200 ml apple juice
Cinnamon
50 gm raisins
Caster sugar to taste.

Method:
1/ Set the oven to 200°c, mark 6.

2/ Melt the butter in the water. When boiling add the flour and beat strenuously for 2 minutes over a gentle heat. Tip out into a large mixing bowl. After about 5 minutes beat in the eggs, one at a time, giving it some welly.

3/ Using a plastic scraper, transfer the paste into a piping bag and pipe out little whirls onto a baking tray. Bake in the oven for about 25 minutes. The shell should be quite firm to the touch; if pliable return to the oven to bake a little longer. Finally, place on a cooling wire.

4/ Peel, quarter and core the apples. Dice finely. Place in a pan with the juice, cinnamon, sugar and raisins. Cook under cover till the apple is softened, but not a purée. Turn out to cool.

5/ With a sharp vegetable knife, cut half way across each choux bun so that they can be opened. Gently spoon in some yoghurt, followed by the apple mixture. Decorate with mint leaves.

6/ This dish can be served with a red plum sauce. Pit a pound of plums. Simmer in a little apple juice to coat the base of the pan. Sweeten with honey or caster sugar. When softened, pass the plums through a liquidiser.

~ ~ ~ ~ ~ ~ ~ ~ ~ ~ ~ ~ ~ ~

## *Banana Bread*

This is an ideal recipe for bananas which look past their best, but are in fact at their sweetest. One cold, miserable day when the world had deserted the seafront, a legless man on a skateboard wheeled into 'The Cook & Fiddle' and ordered mushroom omelette, then banana bread which he wolfed down off a chair. In the absence of a witness no one has ever believed this tale of an old Brighton sea dog washed up by the storm.

Ingredients: (1 loaf)
4 ripe bananas
2 eggs
225 gm wholemeal flour
1 teaspoon baking powder
1 heaped teaspoon of cinnamon
60 ml clear honey

Method:
1/ Set the oven to 190°c, gas mark 5. Brush a loaf tin with oil, line it with greaseproof paper, and brush that with oil again.

2/ Beat together the eggs and honey in a large bowl. Chop the bananas very small and beat together with the eggs and honey.

3/ Sieve the flour, baking powder and cinnamon onto the banana mixture, returning the bran to the bowl. Beat together well.

4/ Scrape out into the loaf tin and bake for 40 minutes, or

until a sharp knife comes cleanly out of the centre of the loaf.

5/ Allow to cool a little and serve. If eaten cold, spread with butter.

~ ~ ~ ~ ~ ~ ~ ~ ~ ~ ~ ~ ~ ~ ~

## *Crêpes Suzette*

The variety of sweet crêpe fillings is endless. Fresh crêpes spun with honey and served with a squeeze of lemon is a simple treat. Paynes Farm at Hassocks has a wide range of blossom scented honey. Another excellent product is fruit yoghurt from the High Weald Dairy. Spoon into folded crêpes, place for 5 minutes in a low oven, and coat with fresh strawberry coulis. Alternatively, envelop spoonfuls of Willetts Farm ice cream inside each crêpe, and serve with a fruit coulis. A real indulgence is Crêpe Suzette, so here is the favourite recipe of Maggie, our trusty dish washer.

Ingredients for 4 people
8 crêpes (see veggie crêpe recipe, page 171)
250 ml orange juice
50 gm caster sugar
50 gm butter
50 ml Grand Marnier
50 ml Brandy

Method:
1/ Fold the pancakes, two to a plate and put in the bottom of a low oven.
2/ Melt the butter and sugar in orange juice. Continue cooking at a high heat, and when most of the liquid has evaporated add the brandy and Grand Marnier. The alcohol should burst into flame. Pour over the crêpes and garnish with a twist of orange.

~ ~ ~ ~ ~ ~ ~ ~ ~ ~ ~ ~ ~ ~ ~

# Local Good Food directory

An amazing number of artisan food producers have emerged in Sussex over recent years. Below is a list of suppliers the Mule can recommend from personal experience.

**High Weald Dairy**. Organic cheeses, mainly from sheep's milk. Soft creamy Sussex Slipcote, firm fulsome Duddleswell, smoked Ashdown Forester, feta and halloumi. The farm also distributes other cheeses from the south, such as 'Bishops Blessing' made from buffalo milk.

Mark and Sarah Hardy, Tremains Farm, Horsted Keynes near Haywards Heath.
Tel: 01825 791636

**Twineham Grange**. Once you've tried this cheese you will wonder why you bothered with parmesan.

Rob Bookham, Bob Lane, Twineham, near Haywards Heath. Tel: 01444 881394

**Coombe Farm Dairies**. The last remaining local milk producer that is not in the hands of a big conglomerate.

Peter van Breda, Westfield Avenue North, Saltdean. Tel: 01273 303998

**Turners Dairies**. Low fat yoghurt, fromage frais and

Greek style yoghurt.

Ray Spears, Myrtlegrove Farm, Patching, Worthing. Tel: 01903 871520

**Willetts Farm Dairy**. Dairy ice cream to die for. Comes in 15 different flavours.

Robin Ashby, Blacham, near Tunbridge Wells. Tel: 01892 740747

**Oaks Poultry Farm**. Chicken, duck, geese and turkey as well as carcass meat butchered on the farm. Also a selection of homemade sausages.

Mark Perrett, Hassocks north of Ditchling. Tel: 01273 843235

**Plantation Pigs**. Located just north of Sussex, Plantation Pigs are free range happy snorters providing extremely tasty meat. Available from a few specialist butchers such as Archers. Hams are distributed to the catering trade through Southover Foods.

Hugh Norris, Shackleford, Surrey. Tel: 01483 810113

**The Weald Smokery**. Serving the top end of the market with caviar and freshwater eel. Also smoked fish, goose, venison and Toulouse sausage.

Mr. Wickham, Mount Farm, Flimwell. Tel: 01580 879601

**Springs Smoked Salmon**. Every variety of smoked fish and seafood.

Martin Harris, Edburton, Henfield. Tel: 01273 857338

**The Merchant Farmer**. Rumpy cider marmalade, hop'n garlic mustard, hot and creamy horseradish. Not to forget their very special fudge.

Jonathan Ffrench, Newbury Cottages, Newbury Lane, Cousley Wood, Wadhurst. Tel: 01892 783430

**Sussex Farmhouse**. Hot Indian rhubarb chutney, Sweet Sussex pickle and Onion marmalade are some of the condiments on offer. Also an extensive range of fruit preserves and pies.

Barbara Pelling, Old Forge, Moor Lane, Westfield. Tel: 01424 754101

**Paynes Farm**. A wide selection of honeys, as well as beeswax and honeycomb. Also a delicious honey and herb salad dressing.

Paul Payne, Wickham Hill, Hassocks. Tel: 01273 843388

**The English Wine Centre**. Stockists of all Sussex wines as well as their own 'Cuckmere Valley'. Generous tasting's and excellent advice offered.

Christopher Ann, Alfriston, just off the A27. Tel: 01323 870164

**Middle Farm**. Offers a wide range of local produce. Also a link with the old tradition of apple growing in Sussex; they hold a special Apple Weekend in December.

Helen Marsh, West Firle, A27 near Alfriston. Tel: 01323 811411

**Ringden Farm apple juice**. Twenty six varieties of apple across the spectrum from sweet to sharp. Every name doubtless tells a tale; 'Laxton Fortune', 'Howgate Wonder', 'Ida Red' and 'Jonagold'.

Chris Dench, Hurst Green, Etchingham. Tel: 01580 879385

**Brighton food shopping list**.
For quality pastry at an affordable price, 'The Real Patisserie' at the top of Trafalgar Street. For bagels, inevitably 'The Bagelman' of Bond Street, six types of bagel with 101 fillings. For good wholesome bread, it is worth a trek uphill to 'The Raven Bakery' at Fiveways. Opposite is 'Fiveway Fruits', a first class greengrocer. For organic meat and local game try 'Archers' in Islingword Road. For local fish visit Neil at 'Sea Haze', opposite the shellfish barrow on the Old Ship Beach. Always a fishy tale to accompany the filleting.

'Infinity Foods' in the North Laines has a great range of organic groceries, all reasonably priced. Just try to cocoon yourself from the whining women, who gridlock the aisles with ermine-lined prams filled with soya milk sadness. 'The Taj' is a relative newcomer, serving an eclectic mix of kosher gherkins, Sussex cheeses and Eastern delicatessen. A wonderful food folly in the mould of the Royal Pavilion. Find it opposite Waitrose on Western Road. More recently a Turkish Deli has lifted the Lewes Road out of food desert status. Tahini, tabbouleh, a Turkish delight. More recent still is 'Sussex and the City'. Duncan Innes, former Maître D at 'Moshi Moshi', takes the concept of a farmers market and locates it in a shop in Meeting House Lane.

For total indulgence try 'Montezumas' chocolate in Duke Street. Everything organic, locally made and flavours like geranium and orange. If you're off for a day at the races, call in at the 'Wild Cherry' deli on Queens Park Road. Then select a rare vintage at tha 'Butlers Wine Cellar', arriving in style astride a mule, champagne corks popping!

Recommending eating out becomes more difficult as places come and go and food is a matter of personal taste. The whole of world cuisine can be found in Brighton, but here are just three recommendations based on value for money. 'Café Motu' at the bottom of Trafalgar Street is like a warm and friendly capsule of Brighton life. The 'lentejas', a Spanish stew of lentils, vegetables and chorizo sausage, will keep you going for a week. Real food and real ale at the bustling 'Basketmakers' in Gloucester Street. Novel daily specials such as crunchy sweet potato pie. Opposite the West Pier, 'The Regency Fish Restaurant' is big and busy with a view of 'The Grand Old Lady'. More importantly, the fish is sweet and the chips chunky. Once I was sat there, chomping happily away, when Sam the lobster man came through with a basket of shiny crustaceans. Real, live and native.

***

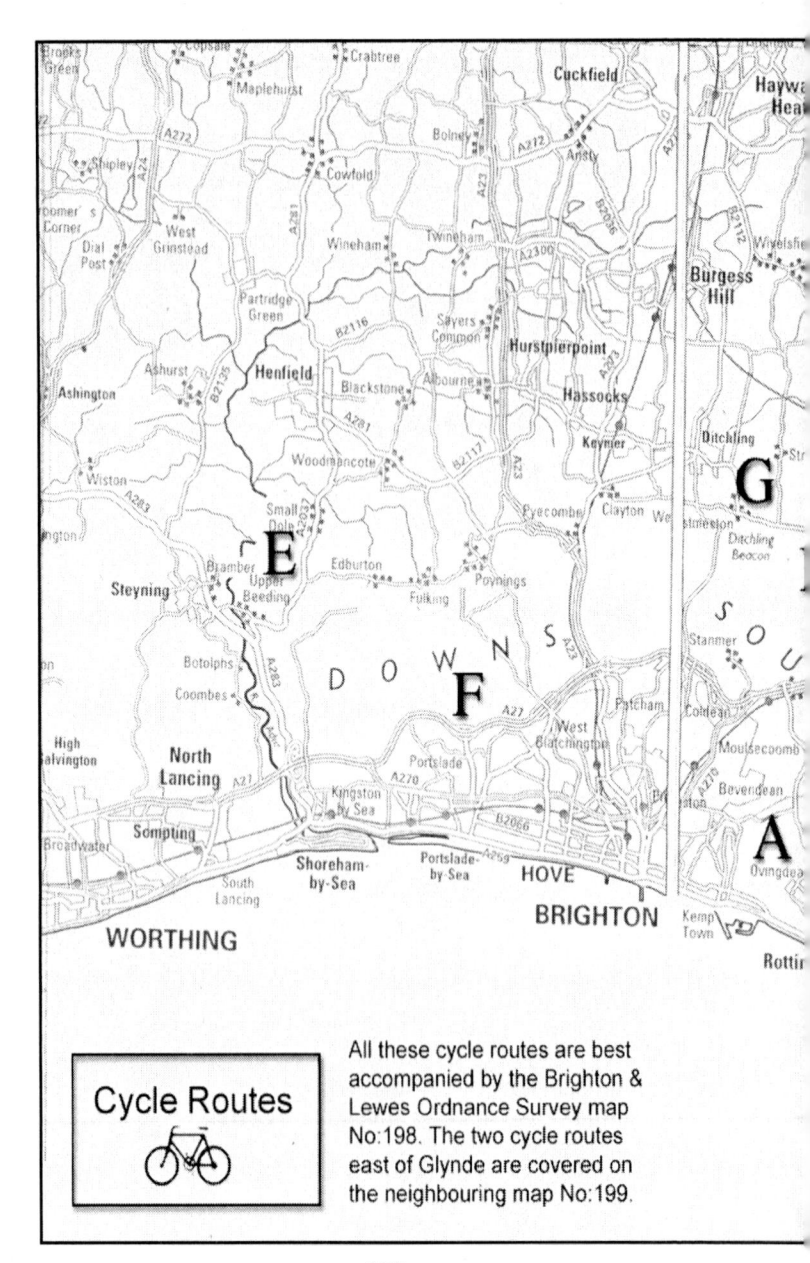

## Cycle Routes

All these cycle routes are best accompanied by the Brighton & Lewes Ordnance Survey map No:198. The two cycle routes east of Glynde are covered on the neighbouring map No:199.

192

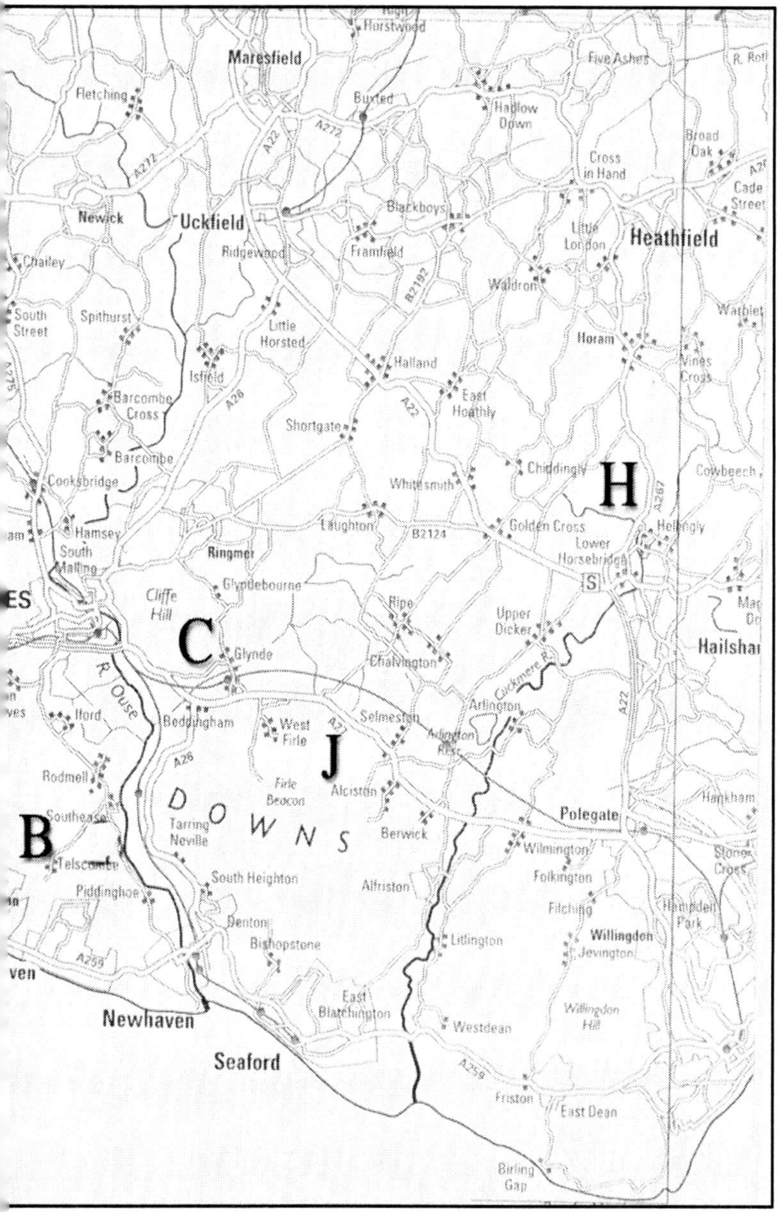
Horstwood
Maresfield
Five Ashes
Fletching
Buxted
Hadlow Down
A272
A22
Broad Oak
Cross in Hand
Cade Street
Newick
Uckfield
Blackboys
Little London
Heathfield
Chailey
Ridgewood
Framfield
B2192
Waldron
South Street
Spithurst
Little Horsted
Horam
Isfield
Halland
Vines Cross
A26
Barcombe Cross
East Hoathly
Shortgate
Barcombe
Chiddingly
H
Cooksbridge
Whitesmith
Cowbeech
A267
Hamsey
Laughton
B2124
Golden Cross
Hellingly
South Malling
Ringmer
Lower Horsebridge
Glyndebourne
Cliffe Hill
Ripe
S
Upper Dicker
C
Glynde
Chalvington
Hailsham
R. Ouse
Cuckmere R.
Beddingham
Arlington
West Firle
Selmeston
Iford
A22
J
Rodmell
Firle Beacon
Alciston
Southease
DOWNS
Polegate
Hankham
Tarring Neville
Berwick
B
Wilmington
Telscombe
South Heighton
Folkington
Piddinghoe
Alfriston
Filching
Hampden Park
Denton
Willingdon
Bishopstone
Litlington
Jevington
A259
Newhaven
East Blatchington
Willingdon Hill
Westdean
Seaford
Friston
East Dean
Birling Gap

# Cycle Routes

**Cycle route A**: Brighton via the Racecourse to Rottingdean. Return along the Undercliff path.

Cycle up Elm Grove, and just before the garden centre at the top of the hill, take the little tunnel under the racetrack. Follow the hoof prints until the racecourse turns off towards the sea. Cycle into Woodingdean; turn left at the crossroads and right onto the bridleway that skirts round the town. This is a firm dry path even in winter, that curls round to Rottingdean. Take the Undercliff path back to Brighton.

Refuelling points: 'Elm Grove Cafe', Brighton. Bubble and squeak breakfast, roasts with umpteen veg.

'The Sea Spray' on the slip road to Rottingdean beach. Ice cream and excellent coffee.

**Cycle route B**: Continuation from Rottingdean to Lewes, via Telescombe Cliffs and the River Ouse.

Take the Undercliff path to Saltdean, pass under the road to the swimming pool and cycle east on the A27 to Telescombe Cliffs. Turn left along the bridleway, and carry on down to Rodmell. Pass through the village till you reach the river, and turn left along the raised embankment. There is a wonderful feeling of freedom and space as the plain spreads out beneath three ranges of The Downs. The river eventually brings you to Lewes. Trains run every fifteen minutes to Brighton.

Refuelling points: 'The Abergavenny Arms', Rodmell. The name is a mystery for a local Sussex pub, but good food is served beside a roaring fire.

'Beckworth's Deli', Lewes High Street. Tasty slabs of homemade pizza.

**Cycle route C.** Newhaven to Glynde, The Happy Camel and Lewes.

Take the train to Newhaven Town station, and cycle through the northern part of the town, up into the hills. You come to a panoramic view of the sea, the river and The Downs. After the radio mast, there is a helter skelter descent to Glynde. Cycle through the village, and in about a mile there is a field of alpaca llamas. On the left is a paddock with the camel. Climb the path to Mount Caburn and continue to the golf course above Lewes. A steep narrow road takes you down to The Cliffe.

You can return to Brighton by train or bike. The cycle track on the A27 is not very pleasant as it runs alongside pounding traffic. A more picturesque journey is described in Route D.

Refuelling point: 'The Trevor Arms' at Glynde, with a big sunny garden.

**Cycle Route D.** Lewes via Mount Harry to Falmer and Brighton.

Cycle up Lewes High Street, and turn right at the lights just before the prison. Almost immediately there is a bridleway on the left, that circles round, past a stable to Mount Harry. Carry on slightly downhill, until you reach a crossroads of paths. Turn left, and when the path eventually divides take the right fork. You pass through some farm buildings, and then hit a tarmac road that runs down to Falmer.

<u>Refuelling point</u>: 'The Swan' at Falmer, excellent soup and real ales.

**Cycle Route E**. Shoreham to Upper Beeding, returning via the airport.

The coastal road from Brighton is thick with thundering lorries, so it is best to take the train to Shoreham. Cross the railway tracks, take the first left and cycle out of town, across the bridge over the A27. The hill is punishing but the view is terrific. Drop down to Upper Beeding, cycle through the village and turn left along the eastern bank of the River Adur. Eventually, you have to join the A283 for half a mile, but soon there is a cycle path off on the right, with big happy sculptures. Once on the outskirts of Shoreham, turn right over the rickety wooden bridge across the estuary. Cycle round to the airport terminal, an art deco building that is well worth a visit. Leave via the road under the railway tracks, and visit Shoreham beach, a peaceful vista of the English seaside. Return along the houseboat towpath and pedestrian bridge.

<u>Refuelling</u>: 'The Bridge Inn' at Upper Beeding. Good food and Badger beer.

The stylish airport café, with an unblemished view of take off and landing.

'Le Grand Fromage' at Shoreham. Decent coffee and excellent cheese.

**Cycle Route F**. Portslade to Devil's Dyke.

Devils Dyke is one of the wonders of the world; the

extent of the view is awesome. You can get there by simply following Dyke Road out of town, but this is a relentless grind shared with traffic. More peaceful to meander through Portslade village, and then make for the hills. I cycled to the Dyke last midsummer for a solstice firework display. Arrived to find I had got the wrong day, but all was not lost. A deep twilight blue enveloped the Dyke, creating an aura of tranquillity. Cycling home, a big lazy moon hung on the horizon, smouldering above the sea.

Refuelling. It is worth exploring Fulking in the valley. 'The Shepherd and Dog' comes recommended by Egon Ronay.

**Cycle Route G**. Brighton to Ditchling village.

It is a steep climb to Hollingbury golf course, but then the road undulates gently across the fields. Just after the ring road, turn right into a car park, and follow the path left through a canopy of trees. At the end of the wood, re-join the road to Ditchling Beacon; another breathtaking view. Impossible to attempt the descent to Ditchling Village without a good set of brakes.

Returning to the Beacon by road is tortuously steep, cars snarling at your rear wheel. Better to circle round to Westmeston, cycle through a little wood, then push your bike up the twisting chalk path to the South Downs Way.

Refuelling. 'Dolly's Pantry' in Ditchling village. Tasty little sausages for breakfast, extensive lunch menu and afternoon cream teas. Mind your head on the beams!

**Cycle Route H**. The Cuckoo Trail and Michelham Priory, returning from Berwick station.

Turn right outside Polegate station, right at the roundabout and you meet the Cuckoo Trail, a peaceful, tree-lined path that follows the course of an old railway. Every village en route is worth a visit – Hellingley, Horam and Heathfield. Coming back, take the sign for Michelham Priory, just north of Hailsham. After visiting the Priory, follow the road that skirts a wood before turning to Arlington and Berwick station.

Refuelling: 'The Dinkum' at Polegate. Hearty portions, reasonably priced; Harveys Best Bitter.

The café at Michelham Priory, with bread made from wheat ground at the old water mill.

The village shop at Berwick station; perfect supplies for a picnic.

**Cycle Route J.** Continuation from crossroads south of Berwick station, up Bo Peep Lane to the South Downs Way and Alfriston.

Cross over the A27, and take a little path across the fields to visit Charleston Farmhouse. Return to Bo Peep Lane, which climbs up to the South Downs Way. From there you can circle round to Alfriston, or carry on to Cuckmere Haven. Return to Brighton from Berwick station.

Refuelling: Alfriston is a picture postcard of English eateries. Midway between there and Berwick station, the English Wine Centre produces a quality line in ready meals to take away.